Canyons, Coves & Coastal Waters

Choice Canoe and Kayak Routes of Newfoundland and Labrador

Dan Murphy
Jim Price
Kevin Redmond

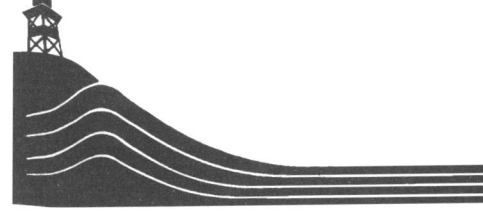

BREAKWATER

BREAKWATER
100 Water Street
P.O. Box 2188
St. John's, NF
Canada, A1C 6E6

The publisher acknowledges the financial contribution of The Canada Council which has helped make this publication possible.

Cover photo by Mark Gerin. Authors photos (back cover) by Kevin Redmond, Mark Dykeman and Harry Butt, respectively.

Canadian Cataloguing in Publication Data

Redmond, Kevin.

Canyons, coves and coastal waters

Includes bibliographical references.
ISBN 1-55081-101-0

1. Canoes and canoeing — Newfoundland — Guidebooks. 2. Kayaking — Newfoundland — Guidebooks. 3. Newfoundland — Guidebooks. I. Price, Jim, 1947- II. Murphy, Dan, 1953- III. Title.

GV776.15.N5R53 1995   797.1'22'09718   C95-950100-2

A portion of the royalties from the sale of this book will be donated to the Protected Areas Association of Newfoundland and Labrador (PAA) to assist in the establishment of parks and reserves. For more information on the Protected Areas Association, write Box 1027, Station C, St. John's, NF, A1C 5M5 or phone/fax (709) 726-2603.

PROTECTED AREAS
ASSOCIATION
OF NEWFOUNDLAND & LABRADOR

Acknowledgements

We would like to thank the following people for their great assistance in making this book a reality: Joe Agnew (Canadian Recreational Canoeing Association), Charlie Banfield, Linda Bartlett, Aneil Beersing, Bob Budgell, Anna Buffinga, Dan Chassion, Mark Dykeman, Sophia Fowler, Brian Green, Keith Guzzwell, Rolf Kraiker, Kevin McAleese, Newfoundland and Labrador Department of Tourism and Culture (Parks Division), Angela Murphy, Roger Pearson, and Margie Price.

These people gave so willingly of time and effort to enhance the quality and completeness of many sections. Maps, photos and waterflow information were gladly donated along with other supplementary information about trip logistics, access and much more. We would like to thank our wives for their understanding of our desire to partake in these often extended paddling trips when, at times, we were needed at home.

To the paddling fraternity and those we have had the privilege of paddling with: your camaraderie and various contributions helped make trips enjoyable and memorable. Without you, this book would not have been possible. We thank you all!

Many thanks to the Breakwater staff—especially John Andrews, Heidi Cramm, Nadine Osmond and Laura Woodford. Your professionalism, commitment and ability to get the job done is very much appreciated.

Kevin Redmond

Exploits River.

Table of Contents

Newfoundland and Labrador is the eastern edge of Canada's frontier. For the most part, it is remote, rugged, pristine and far enough away from the rest of North America to carry a pioneer spirit and unspoiled beauty. There are few areas in the province that have been subjected to overuse. Paddlers who frequent this part of Canada are rewarded not only with its natural beauty but also a spiritual awareness of their surroundings.

Newfoundland and Labrador is one of the few areas in North America that has unspoiled wilderness. The coastal waters and the rivers are corridors to these otherwise inaccessible wilderness areas. As paddlers in this vast wilderness playground, it is important to remember that we are privileged visitors and, therefore, have a responsibility to respect the land and to leave as little impact as possible.

It is our wish that paddlers will help promote and preserve the natural environment so that our children and our children's children will have the same opportunity as we do to paddle this beautiful province.

> What would the world be, once bereft*
> Of wet and of wildness: Let them be left,
> O let them be left, wildness and wet,
> Long live the weeds and the wilderness yet.
>
> — Gerard Manley Hopkins, "Inversnaid"

* lacking

Looking east across Western Brook Pond.

Kevin Redmond

The planning of any wilderness trip requires considerable research that goes beyond the scope of the information contained in this guide. The purpose of *Canyons, Coves and Coastal Waters* is to provide a general overview of the more popular canoe and kayak routes in Newfoundland and Labrador. It is by no means a complete listing of all the possible paddling routes in our province, nor is it a detailed overview of every route. The descriptions included will highlight special or unusual considerations to maximize the guide's effectiveness.

This guide is divided into 3 main sections of text. The first part provides the reader with an overview of Newfoundland and Labrador and serves as a general reference for trip planning, wilderness ethics and safety. Those who are experienced and up-to-date with current paddling trends and practices may wish to move directly to the route descriptions portion of the book beginning on page 32.

The second section contains descriptions of 56 of the more popular paddling routes in Newfoundland and Labrador. The route descriptions have been organized into 4 regions: Eastern, Central, Western and Labrador, and follow a format similar to the one described below.

The following icons represent the types of river crafts discussed in this book. One or two icons will be found at the top of each river section to indicate which crafts are best suited for the area.

| Flatwater Canoe | River Canoe | Whitewater Kayak | Sea Kayak |

RAPIDS: A range of difficulty ending with the most difficult rapids you will encounter (see International River Classification Scale on page 23).

WATER NOTES: A brief note classifying the river and/or describing paddling conditions (winds, currents or major hazards), or emphasizing special circumstances.

DISTANCE: The approximate route length given in km and mi.

DURATION: The time required for a paddler with average paddling ability to complete the route.

FLOW RATE GRAPH: For rivers that are monitored by the Department of the Environment, Water Resources Division, a bar graph displays the flow rate to the river for the paddling season (April-October) expressed in cubic metres per second.

DESCRIPTION: A brief description of the route from the authors' perspective.

LOGISTICS: Put-in(s) and take-out(s) are described in detail.

MAP(S): The map numbers refer to the 1:50,000 Canadian National Topographic Map Series unless otherwise noted.

CHART: For coastal paddling routes, the appropriate navigation charts are listed.

The third section of this book contains an appendix of resource materials and addresses to help you plan your trip. An overview of the Ecoregions of Newfoundland and Labrador can be found at the end of this guide in Appendix 6, page 121.

Kevin Redmond

Glorious shores of Newfoundland.

> The huge island stands, with its sheer, beetling cliffs, out of the ocean, a monstrous mass of rock and gravel, almost without soil, like a strange thing from the bottom of the great deep, lifted up, suddenly, into sunshine and storm, but belonging to the watery darkness out of which it has been reared.
>
> — R.T.S. Lowell

This is how the novelist R.T.S. Lowell described the island of Newfoundland in the 1840s. Described by some as "the Rock" and others as "the last wilderness," Newfoundland and Labrador is an adventurer's paradise. The province, comprised of 111,390 km² (43,000 mi.²), is located off the east coast of Canada in the Gulf of St. Lawrence and is caressed by the arms of the Labrador current from the north and the Gulf stream from the south. To the northwest, on the mainland, lies another 294,330 km² (113,641 mi.²) of a land called Labrador. The distance between the northernmost tip of Labrador and the most southerly point on the island of Newfoundland is a staggering 1,500 km (932 mi.).

With an approximate population of 520,000 residents concentrated in or near the larger communities, there is plenty of space to roam on the island portion of the province. Labrador is sparsely populated along the east coast and inland on the western edge next to the Quebec border, leaving predominantly virgin wilderness in the northern and central regions.

With a rich history going as far back as the Vikings and Basque whalers and a culture distinctive in its own right, this land offers the wilderness traveller an opportunity to explore a history and culture unique to North America. One can still find communities where traditional lifestyles and family values remain, long lost in other parts of the world in the hustle and bustle of twentieth century life.

Getting Ready

Paddling Gear

Make sure everyone has functional paddling gear to suit the trip. All canoes and kayaks should be fitted with a standard set of safety equipment which should include: grab loops, painters, lining ropes (canoe), throw bags, along with adequate flotation devices (in case of an upset) and self-rescue equipment. Spare paddles should also be readily available when needed.

A properly fitting Personal Flotation Device (PFD) should be worn at all times and a helmet should be worn in severe white water or when kayak surfing on the ocean. Consider wearing appropriate clothing—a wet or dry suit if the water is cold or, in more moderate conditions, warm layers of clothing under rain gear.

Remember that all trips do not always go according to plan. Always carry enough gear, including a change of clothes, to take care of an emergency situation. Even on a day trip, it may be wise to throw in some extra food, a full change of clothes and overnight camping equipment just to be on the safe side.

Newfoundland and Labrador Facts at a Glance

- The province has an area of 405,720 km² (156,000 mi.²).
- If it was a U.S. state, Newfoundland would be the fourth largest, behind Alaska, Texas and California.
- With a population of almost 570,000, this works out to less than 2 people per km² (4 people per mi.²).
- It has a total of 17,540 km (10,900 mi.) of coastline: most of it is ideal for paddling.
- There are 34,000 km² (13,140 mi.²) of freshwater lakes and ponds, many teeming with fish such as speckled, brown and lake trout, as well as ouananiche, pike and Atlantic salmon.
- Newfoundland has a moose population approaching 200,000.
- Labrador has the largest caribou herd in the world—the George River herd, which has between 400,000 and 600,000 animals. Insular Newfoundland has over 50,000 caribou, including the Avalon herd which is the most southerly caribou herd in North America.
- With a population of 30,000 people, there are 20 caribou for every man, woman and child in Labrador.
- The world's largest Atlantic murre colony can be found on the Funk Islands.
- North America's second largest murre colony resides in the Witless Bay region.
- The world's largest and second largest Leach's storm-petrel colonies are in Baccalieu and Witless Bay.
- Witless Bay and Baccalieu are the homes of the continent's largest and second largest puffin colonies, respectively.
- The continent's second, third and fourth largest gannet colonies are in Cape St. Mary's, Baccalieu and the Funk Islands, respectively.
- The world's most southerly thick-billed murres are in Cape St. Mary's.
- North America's largest razorbill colony is located throughout the Gannet Islands.
- The waters surrounding the province teem with the world's largest concentration of humpback whales.

How To Get There

Travelling to Newfoundland and Labrador is not as difficult as it seems. Even the remote region of Labrador is serviced by major airlines and coastal boats which run on a regular basis (weather and ice conditions permitting).

The Island of Newfoundland

By Car: After following the Trans Canada Highway east across Nova Scotia to North Sydney, you must take the ferry across the Gulf of St. Lawrence.

By Ferry: Marine Atlantic operates between North Sydney, Nova Scotia and Port aux Basques, Newfoundland twice a day during most days in the summer and once daily during the rest of the year. (Crossing time is 5-6 hours.) Port aux Basques is on the western side of Newfoundland and approximately 905 km (562 mi.) from St. John's, the easternmost tip of the island. During the summer, a 12-hour ferry runs from North Sydney to Argentia in eastern Newfoundland, 130 km (81 mi.) from St. John's. The ferries contain restaurants, movies, comfortable seats, cabins and a bar if you want to wet your whistle. Reservations should be made well in advance, especially with the Argentia service.

By Air: Air Canada and Canadian Airlines International operate a regular service that connects with most major centres in North America and Northern Europe. Air Atlantic and Air Nova provide service between the Atlantic provinces and convenient air travel between points within the province.

Labrador

By Car: Labrador is accessible by car and passenger ferry from St. Barbe on the Northern Peninsula of the island of Newfoundland, or by road from Baie Comeau, Quebec.

By Ferry: There is a commercial steamship service operated by Marine Atlantic from Lewisporte, Newfoundland to many parts of coastal Labrador. A car ferry also operates on a regular schedule from Lewisporte to Goose Bay.

By Air: Canada's 2 major airlines and regional airlines service Goose Bay with connecting flights via Air Labrador to coastal communities.

Air Charter

Many Newfoundland wilderness rivers are accessible only by float plane. The list on the following page describes the most commonly used aircraft and the loads they can carry. Some air charter companies use planes other than those described in Table 1; ask them for carrying capacities.

There are many combinations of people, gear and loading methods which will affect the cost. If possible, get a quote from the air charter company well before your trip. Most companies will gladly give you details of the fees and services well ahead of time. It is a good idea to get a quote faxed or mailed to you from the air charter company so that there are no surprises on the day of departure.

When multiple trips are required to get people and gear to the river, be sure to send adequate food and camping gear on the first trip. If the plane gets grounded before the second trip, those on the river will thank you. The people left outside can always use a motel. (See Appendix 1, page 116 for Air Charter Companies.)

Aircraft Specifications

Cessna 185
- usual payload 317-363 kg (700-800 lbs.);
- can carry 2 kayaks or 1 canoe externally (on short trips, some companies will carry 3 kayaks);
- costs $2.30-2.50/mi.

Beaver
- usual payload 363-454 kg (800-1000 lbs.)
- can carry 3 kayaks or 2 canoes (some companies may only be willing to carry 1 canoe);
- costs $5.00-5.50/mi.

Turbo Beaver
- usual payload 454-545 kg (1000-1200 lbs.);
- can carry 3 kayaks or 2 canoes (can carry 3 kayaks and 3 people with all their gear inside the plane);
- costs $5.00-6.00/mi.

Single Otter
- usual payload 726-907 kg (1600-2000 lbs.);
- can carry 2 canoes externally or up to 6 kayaks (they can pile them inside). Stacking your canoes by taking out the thwarts or nesting kayaks in canoes may enable you to take more;
- costs $5.00-6.00/mi.

Twin Otter
- usual payload 1200 kg (2600 lbs.);
- can carry a large number of canoes or kayaks up to 16 ft. in length
- costs $9.00-10.00 / mi.

Loaded Cessna.

Outfitters

Newfoundland and Labrador have a number of professional outfitters that cater to the outdoor adventurer. (See Appendix 2, page 117, for a list of outfitters.) Offerings include guided canoeing, rafting, kayaking and backpacking trips to some of the accessible and remote regions of the province. Entry level paddlers may consider a guided adventure, thereby ensuring maximum safety and an enjoyable experience. An enjoyable first experience is sure to bring you back for more, possibly on your own.

If you are considering renting, there are some rental outlets. Although quite limited, they are available in the major centres such as St. John's, Clarenville, Corner Brook and Goose Bay. Many adventure tour operators will not only supply guiding services but will also provide boat and equipment rental, trip and food planning and transportation.

Services

Newfoundland has a wide variety of services to suit all your needs. There are numerous shopping malls, restaurants, motels, hotels, sporting goods stores and other specialty shops. Most are concentrated in the 4 major centres of Corner Brook, Grand Falls-Windsor, Gander and St. John's. Many of the smaller towns have fewer goods to select from, but most of the basic requirements for wilderness trips are available.

Labrador, because of its size and low population, has not developed the service industry as has the island. There are only a few major centres. If you have to make significant purchases prior to your trip, Goose Bay is a logical choice, as it has large grocery stores with a wide variety of fresh and dry food. Several outdoor specialty stores can offer a limited supply of paddling gear. In western Labrador, Wabush or Labrador City are your last chances to make purchases before you head into the wilderness.

Jim Price

An outfitter's display at a trade show in St. John's.

Looking west across Western Brook Pond.

Geology

Before the 1960s, most geologists believed that the continents were stationary. However, exploration of the deep sea-floor showed that new sea-floor was continually being created at oceanic ridges such as the mid-Atlantic ridge as continents, such as North America and Africa, moved apart. This gave rise to the plate tectonic theory.

Newfoundland became important in the development of this theory in 1966 when Professor K. Tuzo Wilson of the University of Toronto postulated that there had been a Proto-Atlantic Ocean in central Newfoundland. Wilson suggested that a collision of Europe with North America closed this ocean and formed the Appalachians Mountain belt. The continents stayed welded together until the early Jurassic time, 2 billion years ago. Then they broke apart to form the present day Atlantic Ocean, which continues to open today. The break, however, did not occur along the same lines of the collision. In North America, it lay just to the east of the Avalon Peninsula, leaving fragments of the old European continent still attached to North America. The Eastern Zone of Newfoundland is one of these fragments.

The rocky coastline of Newfoundland provides a superbly exposed cross section of the Appalachians—the ancient mountain belt caused by the original collision of the 2 continents. These mountains extend for some 3,500 km along the east coast of North America and in Newfoundland they have been famous as a testing ground for the plate tectonics theory of mountain building. As a result, Gros Morne was designated a World Heritage Site by UNESCO in 1987.

Newfoundland's Geological Zones

Rocks on the island of Newfoundland are divided into 3 zones: Western, Central and Eastern. The Western zone has been part of North America for over a billion years and is made up mostly of Precambrian rocks. The other 2 zones are relative newcomers. The Central zone was formed as the 2 continents converged and Ordovician volcanic and intrusive rocks were pushed onto the continental margins. The Eastern zone, as mentioned earlier, was once part of Europe and developed much later in the Precambrian era.

Labrador's rocks are of many ages, but almost all of them are extremely old. Many have passed through at least 2 cycles of mountain building (orogenies) accompanied by metamorphism, as the crustal plates of ancient times alternately crashed together and drifted apart. Similar to the island of Newfoundland, Labrador is divided into geological zones or "structural provinces" according to the orogenies that have affected each area.

The above concepts are clearly demonstrated with plate tectonic maps following page 16.

Kevin Redmond

The earth's mantle exposed, Gros Morne.

Animals

There are 36 indigenous species of mammals found in Newfoundland and Labrador. Not many of these animals are a cause for concern for the wilderness traveller. The animals one may encounter are non-aggressive, making it a relatively safe place to trip. However, animals may respond aggressively if harassed.

There are 2 animals that you should be concerned with—the polar bear and the black bear. The polar bear frequents the coast of Labrador and at times, in the spring, has been found as far south as the Avalon Peninsula on the south-east of Newfoundland. Most polar bears in Labrador retreat with the pack ice during early summer, but a bear will occasionally return on an ice flow drifting south in the Labrador current. When the animal lands on Labrador, it usually heads north along the coast and swims across Hudson Strait to Baffin Island. Such a bear may be hungry and can, therefore, be dangerous and unpredictable. Any confrontation with a polar bear should be avoided at all costs. Polar bears have been seen swimming up to 100 km (62 mi.) offshore and can out-distance a paddler in a kayak!

Black bears are abundant throughout the province. In Labrador, during the last half century, they have moved from the forest into the ecological niche vacated by the barren-ground grizzly. Do not let the black bear's cuddly appearance fool you. As omnivores, they are formidable predators and sometimes aggressive camp robbers. Keep your camp clean and do not leave leftovers lying around. Avoid storing food inside the tent and, if you have to leave food near camp, use a sealed container and place it out of reach. Using a rope, you can suspend food packs from large trees.

When travelling, always give bears a wide berth. Make noises to let them know you are in the country and if you encounter a bear while paddling, take the chicken route on the other side of the river away from the bear, giving him lots of time to retreat. If you are confronted by a bear, the shout-and-act-aggressive approach seems to work.

In the fall of the year, moose can become territorial. The occasional wilderness traveller has been charged by rutting moose—and not because of the person's shapely legs. In general, it is recommended that you keep your distance and respect the wildlife in the area, as it is you who is the visitor.

Caribou on the barrens.

Canyons, Coves and Coastal Waters

Newfoundland in the Middle Cambrian (540 million years ago)

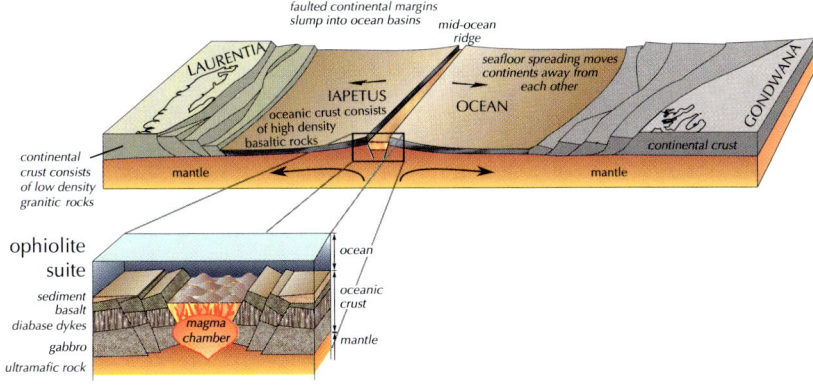

faulted continental margins slump into ocean basins

mid-ocean ridge

seafloor spreading moves continents away from each other

LAURENTIA

IAPETUS

OCEAN

GONDWANA

oceanic crust consists of high density basaltic rocks

continental crust consists of low density granitic rocks

mantle

continental crust

mantle

ophiolite suite

sediment
basalt
diabase dykes
gabbro
ultramafic rock

ocean

oceanic crust

magma chamber

mantle

Newfoundland in the Early Ordovician (490 million years ago)

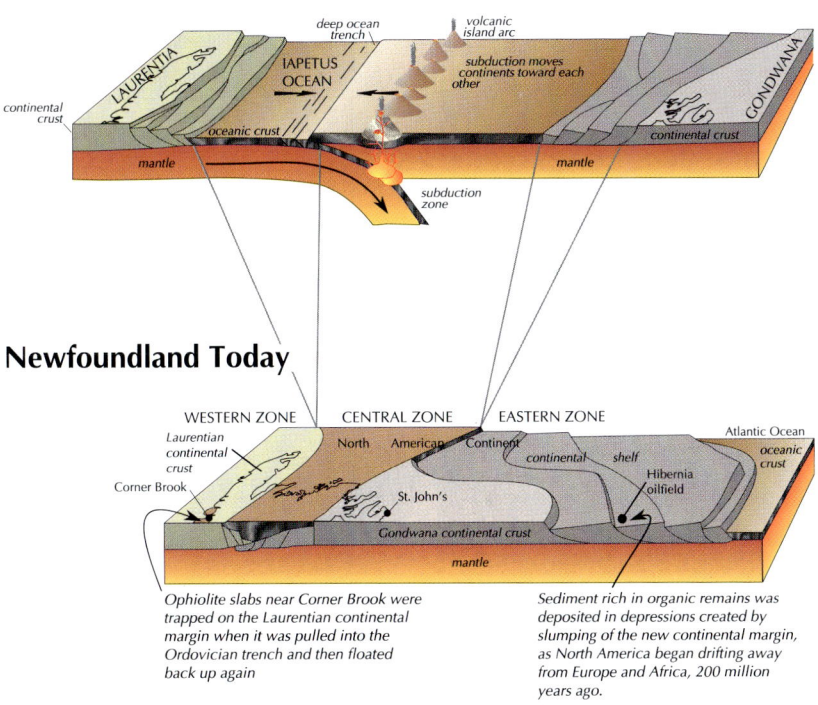

deep ocean trench

volcanic island arc

LAURENTIA

IAPETUS OCEAN

subduction moves continents toward each other

GONDWANA

continental crust

oceanic crust

mantle

mantle

continental crust

subduction zone

Newfoundland Today

WESTERN ZONE   CENTRAL ZONE   EASTERN ZONE

Laurentian continental crust

Corner Brook

North American Continent

continental shelf

Atlantic Ocean

oceanic crust

Hibernia oilfield

St. John's

Gondwana continental crust

mantle

Ophiolite slabs near Corner Brook were trapped on the Laurentian continental margin when it was pulled into the Ordovician trench and then floated back up again

Sediment rich in organic remains was deposited in depressions created by slumping of the new continental margin, as North America began drifting away from Europe and Africa, 200 million years ago.

West Coast shoreline.

Cave in Bonavista Bay.

Near St. Vincent's.

White Bear Bay, South Coast.

Churchill River, Labrador.

Below Gull Island Rapid, Churchill River.

Mount Thorsdby, Port Manvers Run, Labrador.

Kevin Redmond

"Moose crossing" at Bay du Nord.

Sophia Redmond

Camp 6, Deer Lake.

Vegetation

The vegetation of the province varies from tundra in the north of Labrador to mixed coniferous and deciduous forests in western and southwestern Newfoundland to barrens on the Avalon Peninsula. Balsam fir, black spruce and white birch account for 95% of the trees in Newfoundland forests. Approximately 11% of the land surface on the island of Newfoundland and 19% of Labrador are peatlands. Peatlands are concentrated along the coastal lowlands and on the interior high plateaus. Barrens, or heathland, are common in southern Labrador and on the island. Many of the barrens on the island are the result of repeated fires, but the barrens of the Long Range Mountains and northern Labrador are actually classified as tundra.

The beauty of the barrens, bogs and forests of Newfoundland and Labrador is difficult to capture with pen or photo. To sit alone on the barrens and gaze at the distant hills, to walk across an endless bog through a veil of morning mist or to stroll through a Labrador forest carpeted in caribou moss is the only real way to experience this wonderful land.

Reflections: The Pitcher Plant

Whether canoeing or coastal paddling, you are sure to come across a bog during a portage or near your camp site. Bogs are not too hard to find, since 11% of Newfoundland's surface and 19% of Labrador's surface is peat bog. At first encounter, the peat bog looks barren and uninviting, but don't turn back. Take a closer look, and you will discover a most interesting ecosystem.

Kevin Redmond

One of the more interesting plants that inhabit the bog is the pitcher plant—Newfoundland and Labrador's provincial flower. The pitcher-shaped leaves of this plant lure unsuspecting insects to their doom.

The pitcher plant is a carnivorous plant that inhabits nutrient-poor bogs. Insects, lured into the pitcher-shaped leaves, fall into the pitcher and inward-facing hairs prevent them from crawling out. Trapped insects eventually drown and are digested, the nutrients from their bodies supplementing the diet of the pitcher plant.

Within the pitcher of this plant there is a community of living organisms—nematodes, midge larvae and even a species of mosquito that will lay its eggs only in the water trapped in the pitcher of the amazing plant.

Weather

There is an old Newfoundland saying: "If you don't like the weather in Newfoundland, wait a minute." This best describes the Newfoundland weather scene. A recent visitor to the province threw her weather radio away after a couple of days because it had no bearing on what was actually going on outside. It is not uncommon to see 5 weather patterns run in a day. Table 1 shows the average daily temperature in degrees Celsius. These temperatures are long-term averages. Any given day can vary from the norm, especially in areas with their own microclimate such as valleys, mountains or areas affected by the sea. In summer, temperatures can reach 30°C, even in southern, western and central Labrador. The prevailing winds in most areas are from the southwest; however, sudden squalls can come out of nowhere without warning; be prepared. It is not uncommon for backpackers in Newfoundland and Labrador to carry almost the same kinds of clothes in the summer as they do in the winter.

Table 1: Maximum and Minimum Air Temperatures in Newfoundland and Labrador

Month	St. John's		Gander		Stephenville		Happy Valley - Goose Bay	
	max	min	max	min	max	min	max	min
May	10.6	1.9	11.0	1.3	11.0	2.8	9.9	0.0
June	16.5	6.7	17.3	6.2	16.1	7.8	17.0	5.6
July	21.1	11.1	21.9	11.2	19.8	12.2	21.2	10.3
August	20.4	11.6	20.3	10.8	19.8	12.3	19.3	9.2
Sept.	16.5	7.8	15.9	6.9	15.7	8.2	13.7	4.5

Temperatures are in degrees Celsius. More detail about the physical features, climate, vegetation and animals can be found in Appendix 6, page 121: Ecoregions of Newfoundland and Labrador.

Surface Waters of Newfoundland and Labrador

Approximately 8% of the surface of Newfoundland and Labrador consists of fresh surface water, more than any other province in Canada. An additional 11% of the island and 19% of Labrador is wetlands, mainly peat bogs and fens.

On insular Newfoundland, drainage consists of mainly short rivers with small drainage basins. Rocky and shallow soils on the island result in quick run-off. Because of this, many of the rivers are best canoed in late spring and early summer or after long periods of rain. As the season progresses, water levels drop and many rivers become impassable. A day of heavy rainfall can cause rivers to rise considerably. On one occasion, on the Main River, heavy rain resulted in waters of the lower Main River rising a half metre, changing a rather tame set of rapids below the falls into a raging torrent with 1 m (3 ft.) standing waves. By the next morning, the water dropped back to normal, enabling us to continue our journey. Because of the fickle nature of our rivers, plan to canoe them when water levels are at their best.

In Labrador, drainage consists of mainly longer rivers with larger drainage basins. The rivers of Labrador are not as prone to impassable summer levels as those on the island. However, considerable variation in water levels and flow rates may be experienced. On one occasion, the Pinware River rose 2 m (6.5 ft.) in 12 hours: great for the kayakers, scary for the canoeists and a disappointment for the salmon fishermen.

Information about the flow rates of rivers is included in many of the river descriptions in this text. Others can be obtained from the Government of Newfoundland and Labrador, Department of Environment and Lands, Water Resources Division. The department publishes a monthly Water Resources Newsletter which is listed in Appendix 3, page 118: Provincial Government Departments.

Unlike the more southern areas, the water of the larger rivers and lakes in Newfoundland and especially Labrador rarely reach temperatures that are comfortable for a swim. Hypothermia due to immersion should be a major concern even on the warmest summer's day.

Coastal Waters of Newfoundland and Labrador

Newfoundland and Labrador has 17,540 km (10,900 mi.) of coastline. Generally, the coast of Labrador and the eastern and southern coasts of Newfoundland are better suited for coastal paddling because of the many sheltered bays, inlets and fjords that dot the coastline. The west coast of Newfoundland is exposed to predominantly southwesterly winds and lacks many of the sheltered areas found on other coastlines of the province. Despite this, the few sheltered areas on the west coast offer breathtaking scenery and a paddling experience not soon to be forgotten. Surface water temperatures rarely rise above 15°C in the summer months, so come prepared with appropriate wet or dry suits.

Coastal Labrador, Torngat Mountains.

Kevin Redmond

A winter paddle, Middle Cove.

On most of the island, it can be a joy to paddle all year round. Most fresh water is frozen between November and April, but the beautiful blue bays and coastal waters are almost always free of ice. These open waters provide some spectacular paddling, but prudence is essential for pleasure. Frozen waterfalls, giant icebergs, icicles up to 14 m (50 ft.) clinging to cliff faces and cave rooftops are only a part of the scenery a paddler will experience during the "off season." The usual freshwater boating season is April to October and most rivers are at their best April to June and September to October.

Coastal sea ice makes Labrador inaccessible by coastal boat until late spring and sometimes early summer. The breakup of surface waters in Labrador is much later than on the island, occurring generally between May and early June, depending how far north you travel.

Kevin Redmond

You can't miss *all* of the rocks *all* of the time.

If we have a tendency to be critical of the people involved in wilderness accidents, we should maybe remind ourselves that all such accidents could be avoided by simply staying at home.... We know there are risks out there and we know that anyone can make a mistake. It may be an unavoidable mistake or a stupid one. It just makes sense to eliminate the risks as much as we can and learn from the mistakes of others. The physical, mental, and spiritual enjoyment derived from a wilderness journey is worth all the risks.

— Bill Mason, *Path of the Paddle: An Illustrated Guide to the Art of Canoeing*

There is a direct linkage between proper planning, learned techniques, skills, appropriate risk management and the physical, mental and spiritual enjoyments derived from any paddling experience. Unfortunately, back paddling out of a Class 5 rapid is not that easy; avoidance is the key. Many more people have died from being unwillingly swept into a rapid than those who have decided willingly to run the drop. Boat control and the ability to get off the river when you wish are inherent to safe paddling. Judging your own ability, water conditions and weather all play a large role in making the trip free from incident.

Although this book is not a "how to" book on safety, it will touch on some of the more important points on the subject that pertain specifically to the Newfoundland and Labrador paddling experience.

Training and Experience

It is difficult to find in life any event which so effectually condenses intense nervous sensation into the shortest possible space of time as does the work of shooting, or running an immense rapid. There is no toil, no heartbreaking labour about it, but as much coolness, dexterity and skill as man can throw into the work of hand, eye and head; knowledge of when to strike and how to do it; knowledge of water and rock, and of the one hundred combinations water and rock can assume—for these two things, rock and water, taken in the abstract, fail as completely to convey any idea of their fierce embracings in the throes of a rapid as the fire burning quietly in the drawing-room fireplace fails to convey the idea of a house wrapped and sheeted in flames.

— Sir William Francis Butler, *Wild Rivers.*

Canoe and kayak courses are becoming more and more common in even the smaller centres of the country. Training before a trip may ensure that your first canoeing experience is a memorable one. However, you can learn only so much from a course—eventually you have to get out there and do it. This is where you want to know your own abilities as well as the river, lake or ocean in which you paddle. Build up your paddling repertoire slowly by paddling waters of increasing length and difficulty. The key to becoming a good wilderness paddler is your willingness to learn, practice and experience. Remember, there are many courses available to ensure that paddlers keep up with current trends and practices.

Kayak students testing the waters near "Dragon's Throat."

Choosing Your River

Do not bite off more than you can chew when selecting a river—know your limitations and attempt only what you can handle. A leisurely day trip for some paddlers can be a 3-day nightmare for others.

The following considerations should be taken into account when choosing a river: skill level of the weakest paddler, logistics, route length, duration, the waterway's level of difficulty, as well as personal and group equipment.

International River Classification Scale

Class 1: Moving water with a few riffles and small waves. Few or no obstructions.

Class 2: Easy rapids with waves up to 1m (3.2 ft.). Channels are wide and obvious without scouting. Some maneuvering is necessary.

Class 3: Rapids with high, irregular waves that could swamp an open canoe. Narrow passages often require scouting and complex maneuvering.

Class 4: Long, difficult rapids with constricted passages that often require precise maneuvering in turbulent water. Scouting from shore is often necessary and conditions make rescue difficult. Generally impossible for open canoes. Boaters in closed canoes and kayaks should be able to Eskimo roll.

Class 5: Extremely difficult, long and violent rapids with complicated routes that should be scouted from shore. There is a significant hazard to life in the event of mishap. It is essential to be able to Eskimo roll.

Class 6: Difficulties of Class 5 carried to the extreme of navigability. Nearly impossible and very dangerous—for experts who have taken all possible rescue precautions. Serious life risk.

Note: It is an accepted practice to add a grade for wilderness conditions or for cold water. These ratings are purely subjective and change from river to river and from one part of the country to another. It is up to you to take into account factors which least affect the classification.

River Hazards

Most river hazards are minor: a rock just beneath the surface waiting to give you a boost out of your seat if your canoe catches on it; boiling eddies that capsize the unweary; standing waves that bounce a paddler in an unexpected direction or fill the boat with water. Each of these hazards can usually be avoided through anticipation, identification and positive reaction. Errors seldom lead to serious consequences; rather, they are paid for with a roll, a swim or perhaps a boat repair session.

Potentially fatal moving water situations do exist. Exposure to cold water can lead to hypothermia, or hitting your head while swimming can render you unconscious and lead to drowning. The most severe hazards are caused by the current acting in such a way as to entrap or pin the victim under water until drowning occurs. All paddlers must learn to identify these hazards and avoid them wherever possible.

Be alert for waterfalls, holes, sweepers, undercut rocks, continuous rapids and the effects of cold water. Always know what is around the bend. If you are in doubt, pull over and scout from shore.

River Rescue

To make quick and effective rescues, you need training and experience. An emergency situation is a poor place to learn these skills. There are several outdoor centres in North America which specialize in river rescue along with several good books on the subject. One of the best is *River Rescue* by Les Bechdel and Slim Ray (1989, Appalachian Mountain Club Books).

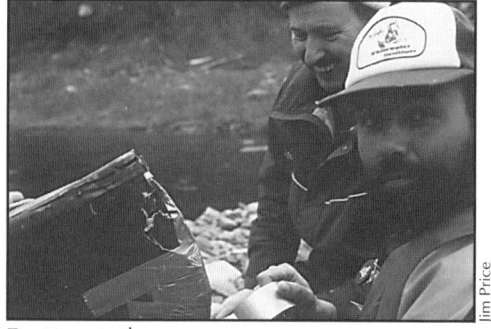

Duct tape to the rescue.

Self rescue is one of the most important skills a canoeist or kayaker can learn. The initial reaction to any threatening situation is to attempt self rescue. Self rescue includes a sequence of procedures that, when executed properly, will deliver the paddler and boat from almost any circumstance. Know how to swim rapids safely and try to practice in controlled settings. Have rescue equipment available and know how to use it.

Lake Hazards

For 4 summers, a group of canoeists paddled from Ontario to British Columbia, retracing Alexander MacKenzie's trek across Canada. During this epic adventure, the group was exposed to all sorts of conditions. When one of them visited Newfoundland, he could not help but notice the continuous windy conditions found here. He commented that he had not experienced anything like it in all his travels. When lake travelling, this should be on your mind at all times as conditions can change very quickly. Cross large lakes early in the morning or late in the evening and stay near shore whenever possible. If windy conditions exist, paddle along the shore since it offers a partial wind shadow.

Another of the major hazards you will encounter is the extremely cold water temperature of our large lakes even in mid-summer. For example, Gander Lake is 274.3 m (900 ft.) deep, has a surface area of 11,500 ha. and a mean water temperature of 5°C with a maximum temperature ever recorded of 17.9°C. Consideration must be given to wind and cold water temperatures when planning your trip.

Ocean Hazards

One of the greatest hazards in ocean kayaking is the inability to go ashore in an emergency situation. Wind, surf and sheer rock walls team up to give long stretches of coastline with no landing zones. As in lake travel, the paddler should be prepared to deal with winds, waves and cold water temperatures. Be prepared to handle capsizes and other emergencies on the water. Other hazards such as overfalls, tidal races and shoals can be identified from charts before setting out.

Navigational hazards in the form of fog or rain storms can occur rapidly. A compass or handheld geographic positioning system (GPS) and chart in these situations is a must. In high traffic areas, larger boats pose a considerable hazard to the unwary paddler.

Special Wilderness Considerations

Plan your trip carefully and follow the plan. Many wilderness travellers consider trip planning to be the most important component of any wilderness expedition. The cause of many wilderness disasters can be traced back to poor trip planning. Be self sufficient and always allow an extra day or two in your plan for unforeseen circumstances. Leave a trip itinerary with local authorities and friends and make sure they know when to send in the cavalry.

Clothing and Equipment

In Newfoundland and Labrador the weather is predictable, that is—it is not uncommon to get the 4 seasons in the 1 day. Therefore, it is important to be prepared for anything. While going down the Churchill River in Labrador, there may be sunshine on one side of the river and thunder and lightning on the other. The further north you travel, the cooler it will get at night. Bring a hat, scarf and mittens no matter what time of year or where you travel. Choose clothing that is either wool or synthetic, since wool retains its insulating ability even when wet and synthetics dry quickly. Remember the scout's golden rule: "Be prepared." The better prepared you are for the foreseen and unforeseen, the more pleasurable the trip.

The high volume of an open canoe allows you to bring considerably more equipment than you would bring on a backpacking or kayaking trip. The type and amount of equipment you carry is directly related to the duration of your trip, the type of country you will be travelling and the season. Heavy loads mean a heavier canoe to paddle and more strenuous portages. It is still best to think "light" when preparing for an extended canoe or kayak trip.

Loading Your Canoe or Kayak

When loading equipment in a canoe, consider the following:

- keep the centre of gravity low by placing heavy items (axes, stove, etc.) on the bottom of the canoe;
- trim your canoe by shifting equipment towards the stern so the bow of the canoe rides slightly higher in the water than the stern;
- place all your equipment in waterproof packs or containers. A large waterproof barrel such as a herring barrel is an ideal container for sleeping bags and personal clothing;
- tie your equipment into your canoe or attach it to a tether.

Kayak touring (ocean and whitewater) is becoming more and more popular. With new boat designs and paddler skill development, people are attempting progressively longer and more demanding trips. Much stems from the paddler's ability to do the magician act, making a mountain of gear disappear into a tiny whitewater boat or sea kayak. This is done not only by bringing just the necessities, but having the lightest gear and food possible. The amount of gear will vary with the length of trip, the difficulty of the rapids and the size of your boat.

When packing equipment for your whitewater kayak, consider the following:

- pack heavy items near the centre or in the bow of your kayak;

- double waterproof all essential gear (which should be all your gear) if you do not have waterproof hatches. Place your gear in a number of small bags rather than one large one. Not only will they better fit into the smaller recesses of a kayak, but you will be able to find things more easily by keeping your food, sleeping bag, clothing and other essential items separate;
- make sure that your spare paddle, camera case and chart case are securely latched on the deck of your sea kayak;
- since a loaded whitewater boat is sluggish, practice in easy rapids first before attempting more challenging ones.

Basic Supplies Checklist

Personal:

- ❑ personal flotation device
- ❑ helmet (white water)
- ❑ flashlight or head lamp
- ❑ matches
- ❑ knife
- ❑ clothing (2 sets)
- ❑ insect repellent
- ❑ sunscreen
- ❑ hat
- ❑ books
- ❑ PHB (personal hygiene bag)
- ❑ treats
- ❑ boots
- ❑ first aid kit
- ❑ jacket

- ❑ personal survival kit
- ❑ maps/compass or GPS
- ❑ water bottle
- ❑ mug & dinnerware
- ❑ sleeping bag & pad
- ❑ footwear
- ❑ bug jacket
- ❑ sunglasses
- ❑ lip balm
- ❑ writing material
- ❑ rain gear
- ❑ camera, film & spare battery
- ❑ fire starter
- ❑ log book
- ❑ extra plastic bags

Canoeing:

- ❑ flotation-paddles & spares
- ❑ spray deck-bailer/sponge
- ❑ duct tape

- ❑ rope
- ❑ repair kit
- ❑ throw bag(s) and other rescue gear

Sea Kayaking Add:

- ❑ paddle float
- ❑ VHF radio
- ❑ dry suit
- ❑ mitts and warm hat-poogies (paddling mitts)

- ❑ flares
- ❑ spare spray skirt (light nylon)
- ❑ charts

Extra Group Equipment:

- ❑ tent
- ❑ cookware
- ❑ first aid kit

- ❑ stove & fuel
- ❑ food
- ❑ toilet paper

Note: Equipment that is used by the group, such as tents and stoves, should be shared evenly among the boats.

Those pesky bugs.

> The flies, which in the Nascaupee country had been such a trial to me, had not driven the men to use veils except on rare occasions, but now they were being worn even out on the lake, where we were still tormented. Backs and hats were brown with the vicious wretches, where they would cling waiting for a lull in the wind to swarm about our heads in such numbers that even their war-song made one shiver and creep. They were larger by far than the Jersey mosquitoes and their bite was like the touch of a live coal. Sometimes in the tent a continual patter on the roof, as they flew against it, sounded like gentle rain.
>
> — Mina Hubbard, *A Womans Way*
> *Through Unknown Labrador.*

The mosquito, jokingly referred to as Newfoundland's provincial bird, is really not as big or voracious as most reports say. A fly net or bug jacket will normally give you ample protection against these buzzing pests. Black flies and no-seeums (sand flies) are a little harder to protect yourself against because they have the unwelcome ability to squeeze in under your net and get you when you least expect it.

Labrador bugs, whether because of the longer fast over winter or the smaller number of available victims, seem to have a much healthier appetite. Bug jackets and fly nets are, again, your best bet with a little fly dope on any exposed skin. If using fly dope, remember that most types break down many materials such as gore-tex , fishing line and sometimes the varnish on your paddle. Deer flies are also a problem in Labrador, so wear a fairly thick shirt—they can bite through T-shirts and polypropylene.

We all know how hard it is to eat or drink through a head net. Your only bastion of relief may be your tent. Make sure the netting and zippers are in good shape.

Because of Newfoundland's variable climatic conditions, the arrival time of the pesky critters may vary significantly. In Newfoundland, mosquitos can be "felt" around late May. Black flies rear their heads a couple of weeks later and both reach their peak around the middle of July. Mid-August sees a decline in all species, but some hardy insects will hang on until late August or early September.

In Labrador, the bug season starts as late as June and can end as early as July or August.

Water Quality

Most Newfoundlanders drink straight from the stream or pond and suffer no ill effects. If you have any concerns, treat, filter or boil the water before drinking. Be especially cautious of water downstream from major towns, cities or industrial development such as pulp mills. If you have any questions on water quality, contact: The Department of Environment and Lands, Water Resources Division, Water Quality Section (see Appendix 3, page 118: Provincial Government Departments).

First Aid

Carry a first aid kit, and know how to use it. As first aid and CPR courses are available at reasonable costs across North America, it would be wise to take these courses before attempting any wilderness trip. Be familiar with the special medical needs of your group and the potential accidents that might occur while travelling. Hypothermia must be watched for at all times. It is progressive in nature and can occur even when the temperature is well above freezing. Prevention is the best cure for any accident; however, if one should occur, know how to treat it.

Firearms

Generally, there is no need to carry firearms on any wilderness trip in Newfoundland or Labrador. Common sense and the ability to avoid potentially dangerous situations is the best defence against wild animals. If you want to bring a gun with you, it is advised that you contact the Wildlife Division or the Royal Canadian Mounted Police.

Communications

Cellular phones, radio telephones and portable ham radios work in many wilderness areas on the island of Newfoundland and in Labrador, but do not depend on them to order out for pizza.

Fishing

Speckled trout and Atlantic salmon are the 2 most prized game fish in Newfoundland. Rainbow, *ouananiche*, Arctic char and brown trout are also fished. In Labrador, the fish are much bigger and more plentiful. There are also lake trout, pike and whitefish which are not available on the island. Non-resident fishing licences are required and on scheduled rivers you will need a fishing guide. Check with the local fisheries officer if you intend to fish on your trip.

Minimum Impact Wilderness Travel

Some of you may ask: "Well, what is minimum impact wilderness travel?" Simply put, it is an attitude combined with a lifestyle which leads to keeping our wilderness a place where others, be it man or beast, can follow in our footsteps and perhaps not even know we were there. To travel in our wildlands means to accept responsibility for preserving them.

Campsites

The further north you go, the more fragile the environment becomes. Scars in northern Labrador may last 100 years, whereas on the island the same scar may last a week. Recognizing these differences and adjusting accordingly is an important component in the preservation of our wilderness.

If camping in a high-use area, it is better to re-use a camping area than choose a new one. Try to leave the site unaltered and carry out ALL your garbage. If the campsite is left in an appealing condition, others will use it rather than a new one.

When camping in pristine or sensitive areas, the most important thing is to begin looking for a campsite early. We have all ended up picking a campsite at dusk or later, not seeing the site till next morning. The object of site selection is to find a durable site which will look the way you found it after you are gone. When camping in areas with sensitive vegetation, re-using campsites is not recommended.

High Use Area

General rules for campfires in high-use areas:

- do not hide your fire pit: leave it so that the next traveller will use the same pit rather than make a new one;
- if you know the site is frequently used, consider collecting dead wood from sites upstream before you stop;
- cook on a stove;
- use what wood you have for the evening camp fire.

Pristine or Protected Area

Make a low impact fire following the steps outlined below:

- carefully remove the litter and duff (black organic soil) to expose the mineral soil (sand and rock);
- lay an old piece of wet canvas on the ground;
- cover the canvas with mineral soil;
- make your fire on top of the mineral soil;
- use only dead wood;
- make sure that ALL the wood is burned to ash;
- before you leave, scatter the cold ash to the wind;
- replace the mineral soil, duff and litter.

Driftwood collection.

Campfires and Stoves

Most wilderness travellers still have an affection for the warmth and sense of companionship that a campfire generates. It is a focal point around which stories are told and plans are made for the next day's paddling or the less popular portage. For some people, the campfire is as good as a friend.

Campfires do, however, leave scars. If you decide to make one, remember the High Use Area and Pristine or Protected Area guidelines on the previous page which will keep the impact on the environment to a minimum.

In recent years, camp stoves have become more popular and reliable, resulting in many back country travellers choosing to carry small stoves or the larger 2-burner stove rather than relying on a fire. Lightness, clean burning and ease of operation have made them the primary choice over the old campfires of the past. In high use areas, dead wood, litter and live trees begin to disappear with successive visitors. Because of this, it is strongly recommended that stoves be used for cooking in these areas.

In an emergency situation, remember to focus on your personal survival rather than your impact on a camp site.

Wilderness Sanitation

Generally, Newfoundland waters are clear and clean. In recent years there has been a heightened awareness of giardiasis, commonly known as "beaver fever." This disease is spread through fecal contamination by both humans and animals. There is an increased use of water purifiers on trips as a preventive measure, even though their use may not be necessary. Many paddlers use them to decrease the risk of the disease.

For most situations the "cat-hole" is the recommended way to dispose of human wastes. Walk into the woods well away from the river or lake and dig a small hole down into the duff (duff is the black soil rich in bacteria). Deposit feces in the cat-hole and, if the soil is moist, burn the toilet paper. Replace the duff and litter. Do not compact—compaction reduces the amount of oxygen available for the bacteria, reducing the rate of decomposition.

A latrine may be required where other methods are not practical, but it does increase the risk of water pollution or animal infestation. It should be dug at least 50 m (160 ft.) from water and 25-30 cm (1 ft.) deep. To increase the rate of decomposition, a layer of soil or vegetation should cover each use and, when you leave, replace ground soil and vegetation. Toilet paper is best burnt or carried out.

In northern Labrador and in parts of Newfoundland, you will be travelling over tundra or barrens where soil cover is sparse or non-existent. In these areas, spread feces with a stick over rock or soil and burn toilet paper.

In coastal areas, it is acceptable to dispose of human wastes below the low tide mark. High levels of bacteria in this area will quickly break down any human wastes and urine will be diluted. Avoid urinating or defecating in or around tidal pools. In high-use coastal areas, it is best to use a cat-hole as outlined above.

When washing in the wilderness of Newfoundland, whether it be dishes, laundry or yourself, it is recommended to avoid soaps. If they are necessary, use a phosphate free soap/detergent and keep it well back from the water. Remember, the sweeter you feel and smell, the bigger the feast the black flies will have.

If you do any amount of back country and wilderness travel, you will encounter garbage. This is unfortunate but the situation is improving as wilderness travellers become more environmentally aware. Remember the old saying to "pack out what you pack in."

Do a sweep check of your campsite as you are leaving to ensure no garbage is left and the site is as good or better than it was when you arrived. In pristine areas, try to leave the campsite in a state where even the most seasoned back country traveller will have difficulty determining if the site was used as a camp.

Wilderness campsite, Main River.

Jim Price

Eastern tip of Bell Island, Conception Bay.

There is something exciting in the first start even upon an ordinary journey. The bustle of preparation—the act of departing which seems like a decided step taken—the prospect of change, and consequent stretching out of the imagination—have at all times the effect of stirring the blood and giving a quicker motion to the spirits. It may be conceived then with what sensation I set forth on my journey.... Before me were novelty and enterprise; hope, curiosity, and the love of adventure were my companions; and even the prospect of difficulties and danger to be encountered, with the responsibility inseparable from command, instead of damping rather heightened the enjoyment of the moment.

— G. Back, *Narrative of the*
arctic land expedition to the
mouth of the Great Fish River.

Jim Price

Tors Cove, Southern Shore.

The air subtle and wholesome, the summer season pleasant…. The land of the north parts most mountainy and woody, very thick of fir trees, spruce, pine…. The greatest part of the plains are marsh and bogs, yet apt to be drawn dry by means of many fresh lakes intermixt which pay tribute to the sea; and on the brinks of these lakes, through which the water drains away for the roots of the grass, it flourisheth. In the other parts of the plains where the water standeth and killeth the growth of the grass with his coldness, it is rushy and sedgy; in some parts barren and mossie ground; but that is firm and dry bearth good grass.

— John Mason's account of eastern
Newfoundland in 1620

For the purpose of this guide, the eastern region of Newfoundland consists of the Avalon Peninsula west to the mouth of the Bay-du-Nord River (but not including it) and north to the eastern boundary of Terra Nova National Park. Most of this region lies within the confines of 3 ecoregions: the maritime barrens, the oceanic barrens and the central Newfoundland forest. Summers are cool on the Avalon Peninsula and warmer as one travels off the peninsula. At one time, much of the Avalon Peninsula was covered with forest; however, most of it has been destroyed by fire and man. Forest can only be found in sheltered valleys. Once off the Avalon Peninsula, the remainder of the region boasts extensive stands of balsam fir, and in areas having survived extensive fire, black spruce dominate. The nature of the coastline, with its multitude of protected bays, makes it an ideal destination for the avid coastal paddler.

There is no shortage of history in this region. St. John's is the oldest city in North America and when the pilgrim fathers landed at Plymouth Rock there were 40 ships anchored in St. John's harbour. With a history going back almost 500 years every community, bay and river has a story to tell.

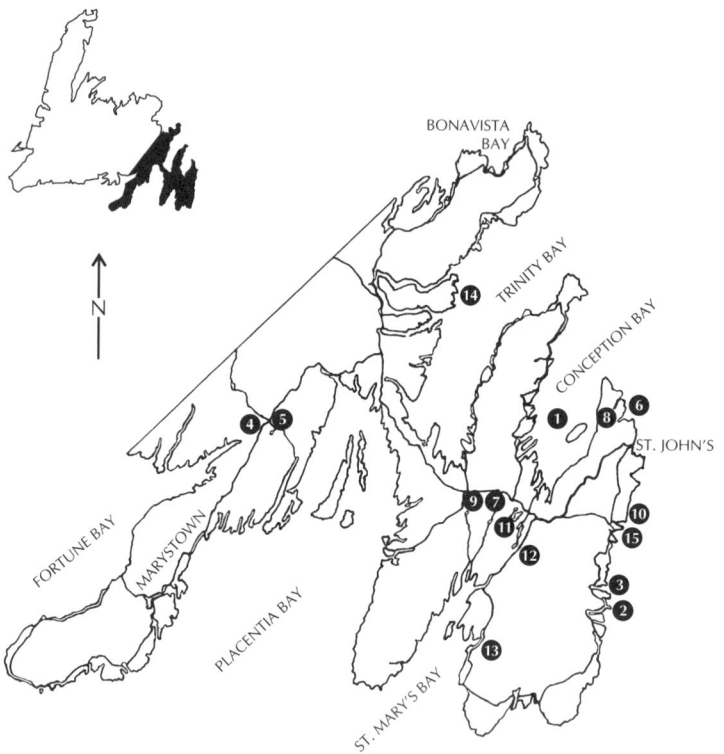

1	Conception Bay	10	Petty Harbour to Bay Bulls
2	Calvert - Ferryland	11	Salmonier Line - Middle Gull
3	Cape Broyle		Pond - Brigus Junction
4	Dunns Brook	12	Salmonier River
5	Paradise River	13	Holyrood Pond
6	Middle Cove	14	Lower Lance Cove - Ireland's
7	Colinet River		Eye Loop
8	Middle Three Island Pond	15	Great Island - LeManche Loop
9	Rocky River		

Conception Bay

RAPIDS: N/A, ocean paddling.

WATER NOTES: For the most part, Conception Bay is sheltered and rarely gets too rough for sea kayaking during the summer months. The exception is a strong northeast wind coming directly in from the sea which can cause moderate swells and sometimes choppy conditions.

DISTANCE: A coastal paddle from Bay de Verde to Cape St. Francis is approximately 200 km (124 mi.). However, there are numerous short trips between the many communities which dot the coastline. Three such trips are:

○ Portugal Cove to Bell Island return 12 km (7.5 mi.);

○ Topsail Beach to Kelly's Island return 20 km (12.5 mi.);

○ Holyrood to Topsail Beach 25 km (15.5 mi.).

DURATION: Although duration will often vary, the following are some estimates:

○ Portugal Cove to Bell Island - 3-4 hours;

○ Topsail Beach to Kelly's Island - 3-5 hours;

○ Holyrood to Topsail Beach - 4-8 hours.

DESCRIPTION: Conception Bay is steeped in history. Every community contains a piece of the past—a famous son, an historic building or the site of a significant event. Many of the scenic coastal communities have an Old World charm which makes the area appealing. Sea kayaking is an ideal way to visit these cultural gems while enjoying the rugged beauty of the marine environment. Care should be taken if venturing past Bay de Verde toward Baccalieu. This island bears witness to the potential menace of the North Atlantic: the wrecks of more than a dozen ships lie under the waters surrounding it.

All distances and times are approximate depending on wind and water conditions combined with the amount of time spent exploring. Much of the coastline surrounding the Avalon Peninsula is free of ice most of the year. When the Arctic pack ice is in the bay (normally early spring), spectacular paddling conditions exist when the sea is still and the wind is calm. The danger that exists with wind or sea swells is that the ice becomes packed together, making it impossible to paddle. The pack ice is made up of ice pans that are small enough to allow you to hop or to dance from one to the other without getting wet, while others are large enough to beach several canoes or kayaks on and to get out to cook a lunch. Conception Bay comes alive at sunrise and sunset. Paddling on a still evening as the sun sets in the west, among the ice pans and the seals, brings a sense of peace and serenity.

In late spring the arctic icebergs, some up to 10 stories high, drift lazily into the bay, sometimes getting grounded and remaining for days or weeks. Paddling through the core of one such iceberg with an archway of ice towering above was irresistible. As we paddled away, a loud cracking noise was followed by a rumble and a splash. The heat of the sun and warm spring breeze melted the top of the iceberg causing the top to crack off and the iceberg to tumble over. Because of their unpredictability, extreme caution should be used when paddling near icebergs.

Summer brings the humpback whale, weighing up to 40 tons to Conception Bay to feed on ground fish such as cod and caplin. When paddling to either Bell or Kelly's Island, remember the dominant wind funnels towards Portugal Cove, which thereby creating a crosswind. A lunch of fish and chips at Dick's Restaurant on Bell Island makes it worthwhile. If conditions deteriorate over lunch, the Portugal Cove-Bell Island ferry can get you back to Portugal Cove. Paddling from Holyrood to Topsail usually brings the luxury of a tailwind and some good surfing.

Although there are only a few specific routes mentioned for this area, paddling any part of Conception Bay has something special to offer.

LOGISTICS: Put-ins and take-outs are much too numerous to mention in this book. Almost every community surrounding the bay has slipways which can be used by kayakers. Shuttles can often easily be arranged by talking to the locals around the wharf or by contacting the nearest tourist chalet.

MAPS: 2C/2, 1N/6, 1N/10, 1N/11, 1N/14, 1N/15.

CHART: 4847.

Pothead whales in Conception Bay.

Calvert - Ferryland

RAPIDS: N/A, ocean paddling.

WATER NOTES: Onshore winds can cause large breaking waves near Stone Island, Goose Island and the other islands in Ferryland Harbour.

DISTANCE: 14 km (9 mi.).

DURATION: 4-6 hours.

DESCRIPTION: This trip offers the opportunity to explore some of the most historical coastlines in the province. After you put-in at the abandoned fish plant near Gut Pond, you head east along the north shore of Calvert Bay. Be careful when passing Stone Island as nasty breakers come out of nowhere from time to time which threaten the unsuspecting paddler with thrashing.

On our last trip there, Joe, a fellow sea kayak guide, was paddling through a narrow channel with high cliffs on either side. We paddled around the seaward side of the small rock island expecting him to be sitting there in the quiet cove waiting for us. Instead, what greeted us was Joe bailing frantically. When we gave him an inquiring look, he said that about half way through the channel he heard a roar behind him. Before he had time to look over his shoulder a giant wave hurled him forward and tossed him end over end, collapsing his spray-deck and half filling his boat with water. He had managed to roll up and was none the worse for his close encounter of the white kind! (We think he is now installing rear view mirrors on his kayak.)

Heading south from Stone Island will bring you past Goose Island and Bois Island which look like overgrown sea stacks. Turn east before Ferryland Head and slip into Ferryland Harbour, site of the earliest continuous colonial settlement in Newfoundland dating back to 1621, when Ferryland was founded by Lord Baltimore. As you make your way back along the west shore of Calvert Bay, you will notice the remnants of several ships washed up on the shores, a solemn reminder of the power of the sea.

LOGISTICS: Take Route 10 to the town of Calvert. Turn left past Old Woman's Pond. The put-in is at the bottom of the hill near the old fish plant.

MAP: 1N/2.

CHART: 4845.

Cape Broyle

RAPIDS: N/A, ocean paddling.

WATER NOTES: Some of the cobble beaches are quite steep, causing dumping waves. When going ashore, send the most experienced in first so they can help other boaters ashore.

DISTANCE: 20 km (12 mi.).

DURATION: 4-6 hours (depending on time spent exploring).

DESCRIPTION: When onshore northeast or southeast winds inhibit your enjoyment on the Southern Shore, Cape Broyle is the place to go. This 8 km (5 mi.) long harbour gives you protection from almost any wind except a straight easterly. On this trip you can paddle through rock caverns, explore sea caves or shower in sparkling waterfalls plunging from the high cliffs—all with the added security of a safe harbour. In June and July, there is a good chance of sighting whales as well as mammoth icebergs that float by.

LOGISTICS: Cape Broyle is located 62 km (37 mi.) south of St. John's on Route 10. You can launch from the slipway on the north side of the harbour, near where the tour boats tie up. Depending on wind conditions, it makes a great loop if you paddle out the north side of the harbour to Admiral's Point and turn south across the harbour to Freshwater Cove where a 20 m (66 ft.) waterfall cascades onto the beach.

MAP: 1N/2.

CHART: 4845.

Sea stacks near Cape Broyle.

Jim Price

Dunns Brook

RAPIDS: Class 2-3 (This is an optional run on the return since you first portage past these rapids to reach the put-in.).

WATER NOTES: This trip is almost entirely flat water. A Class 2 or 3 rapid is portaged going up river to the put-in and may be run on the return back down river if desired.

DISTANCE: 11 km (7 mi.).

DURATION: 4-6 hours.

DESCRIPTION: Dunns Brook offers a welcome alternative to those who are not up to the rigours of intense whitewater as offered by the Paradise River, which Dunns Brook becomes as it crosses the Burin Peninsula Highway. This trip starts with the most bothersome task of a 400 m (1300 ft.) portage before the put-in. A good trail, however, leads from the highway to Dunns Pond just above Entry Falls which is also the start of the Paradise River trip (described next). From here, the travel up river toward Dunns Pond is impressive. Treeless rolling hills give the area a tundra-like appearance. The chance sighting of caribou gives you the illusion that you are in a northern wilderness thousands of km from any road or community. Another short portage at the head of the pond brings you into a beautiful meandering stream, winding its way into the heart of the Newfoundland interior. A little over 5 km (3 mi.) up river, you will encounter rapids. Here is where you can have lunch, do some fishing or explore the surrounding countryside before the return paddle back to the put-in.

LOGISTICS: Dunns Brook is located approximately 30 km (17 mi.) south of the Trans Canada Highway where it crosses the Burin Peninsula Highway (Route 210) and joins the Paradise River. Drive 0.5 km (0.3 mi.) past the bridge and you can see Entry Falls 400 m (1300 ft.) up river to the right. Put-in and take-out are just above this major rapid.

MAPS: 1M/10, 1M/15.

CHART: N/A.

Portage to Dunns Brook.

Paradise River

RAPIDS: Many rapids are fairly steep and best approached with closed boats. They may, however, be run with open canoes properly fitted with thigh straps and plenty of flotation.

WATER NOTES: About half-way down there is a narrow gorge with two 3 m (10 ft.) waterfalls. The first may be runnable but is followed immediately by the other which has a nasty keeper hole at the bottom. This section should be scouted carefully. Give the dam at the end of the trip a wide berth if it is spilling. It is a 40 m (130 ft.) plunge onto a concrete landing pad—not too soft!

DISTANCE: Entry Falls to the hydro dam -19 km (12 mi.).

DURATION: 1-2 days

DESCRIPTION: In 1987, a valiant effort was mounted by the Newfoundland Canoeing Association to save this free flowing river from hydro development. Even with the support of the Wilderness and Ecological Reserves Council, the Canoeing Association was unable to convince the Newfoundland Government to cancel or defer the project. A 20 m (66 ft.) falls and a scenic 40 m (131 ft.) deep gorge, unparalleled in the Province, was flooded and lost forever. Fortunately, the flooding extended only 3 km (1.9 mi.) upstream from the dam, leaving much of the river untouched and available for recreational use.

Entry Falls, a Class 3 rapid, is the normal put-in for either a trip down the river or a day playing on the first kilometre of white water. One km (0.6 mi.) below this rapid the river crosses the Burin Peninsula Highway. Watch out for the 1 m ledge just below the bridge. Two-hundred metres (656 ft.) downstream from the bridge there is a 7 m (23 ft.) waterfall which should be portaged on the left. An easy 4.5 km (2.8 mi.) flat water section follows before the river swings sharply to the right and funnels through a Class 4 or 5 canyon. A fairly easy portage on the right up over a steep embankment will get you around this obstacle. Most of the rapids following this section are runnable although many should be scouted, as visibility from upstream is impaired by the steepness of the gradient, and there are still several exhilarating Class 4 or 5 drops left before the buried rapids of the reservoir pass, silenced, beneath the bottom of your boat.

LOGISTICS: The Paradise River is located approximately 30 km (18.5 mi.) south of the Trans Canada Highway where it crosses the Burin Peninsula Highway (Route 210). Drive 0.5 km (0.3 mi.) past the bridge and you can see Entry Falls 500 m (1,600 ft.) up river to the right. Take-out is at the end of the reservoir on the left where the hydro access road ends. For a shorter trip, you can take-out 7.6 km (4.5 mi.) below the bridge which requires a 0.7 km (0.5 mi.) portage out to Monkstown access road.

MAPS: 1M/9, 1M/10.

CHART: N/A.

Middle Cove

RAPIDS: N/A, ocean paddling.

WATER NOTES: Underwater shoals on the northern tip of the cove can cause large rollers or breakers. Caves should only be entered under calm conditions.

DISTANCE: 2-15 km (1.2-9 mi.), depending on the amount of exploring.

DURATION: 1-10 hours.

DESCRIPTION: A paddle with a difference is the best way to describe this area. As it is so close to St. John's and a popular area to visit, you can be pretty sure that there will be spectators watching your every move—in the event of a capsize, you will be the entertainment for the day.

There is not always a warm-up for this paddle due to the swell (surf). In fact, for some it becomes a quick cool down. In order to get on the water, you must slide the canoe in the water as the surf rolls in. If the timing is not just right, you will end up high and dry in a position for the next wave to dump on top of you and your boat. No matter what time of year you are in the North Atlantic, the water is very cold.

Once off the beach, you may hug the right shoreline and explore a series of caves at the base of a 180 m (600 ft.) sheer cliff face. Approach these caves with caution, as when the swell is up, it is possible to get smashed against the roof of the cave. Of the 5 caves in the south face, one is approximately 60 m (200 ft.) deep while another allows you to land on a beach inside.

During winter months, the rock face and caves are more impressive as you paddle beneath icicles that are up to 15 m (50 ft.) in length (see photo on page 20). In late spring, this area is littered with icebergs, carved from glaciers in the high Arctic and carried southward by the Labrador current.

North from Middle Cove towards Torbay, there are more caves and a nice surfing area called the "Motion." Look for a small concrete and rock hut on shore and a series of rock outcrops just off shore from it. Between the 2 most southerly rocks, a curling wave rises from what seems to be nowhere.

South from middle Cove, there is a coastline dominated by barren rock faces, some jagged, some old and worn. Towards Outer Cove, the sea swells become more prominent. What is relatively calm in Middle Cove can become a roller coaster ride over this way. From Outer Cove, you can continue on to the Marine Lab (Memorial University's marine science research centre), located on the shore of Logy Bay. The centre offers interpreted tours of the marine life found in our coastal waters. For those who have the time and are more adventuresome, it is possible to continue south to Quidi Vidi Village or to St. John's harbour.

When planning your trip along this coast, always monitor the weather conditions, as there are not a lot of places where you can get off the water easily when it gets rough. In addition, there are strong undertows in the area which have resulted in a number of deaths over the years. Even when there is no wind, the sea may be rough with large swells which can be more dangerous than those created by the wind. Your judgement and prudence are crucial.

LOGISTICS: Despite the majesty and pristine nature of this area, this is not a fly-in trip. In fact, it is a 10 to 15 minute drive from St. John's. Follow Route 20 north until you see the turn off for Middle Cove. The beach is on your left, about 3 km down this road.

MAP: 1N/10.

CHART: 4846.

Reflections: The Moose

Despite the large moose population present in Newfoundland today, the moose is not native to our province. The first attempt to introduce moose from Nova Scotia to Newfoundland in the late 1800s was unsuccessful. What is amazing is that the present day moose population, exceeding 200,000 animals, is the prodigy of just two males and two females which were successfully introduced from New Brunswick in 1904.

Kevin Redmond

Newfoundland now has one of the highest moose population densities in North America, such that extreme caution must be taken by motorists from dusk to dawn to avoid moose on our highways. During the summer months, it is not uncommon to see a line of cars hastily parked on the shoulder of the road, all with foreign license plates and a group of tourists out with their binoculars and cameras focused on a moose feeding nearby. The closest look either of us has had was a head-on collision with a 1,600 pound bull moose while driving out to canoe the Exploits River one Thanksgiving Weekend. Destroying the car and canoe, the moose limped away while we luckily hopped out of the car like a jack-in-a-box helplessly looking at the twisted canoe lying in front of the car with half the canoe rack still attached.

The largest member of the deer family, a bull moose stands taller at the shoulder than the largest saddle horse and can weigh close to two thousand pounds. Despite its large size, the moose can be as quiet as a cat in its travels through the thick knitted boreal forest prevalent in most regions of the province. Moose are herbivores and an adult moose eats up to 60 lbs of forage a day, sometimes diving close to 20 ft. to eat plants growing on the bottom of a lake or pond. The moose has an exceptionally good sense of hearing and smell, yet its eyesight is very poor. A beautiful and majestic animal, the moose is likely to play a pleasing part in your travels throughout the province.

Colinet River

RAPIDS: Most rapids are only riffles. At high water, there may be a few short Class 2 runs. At the lower end of Fifth Pond, there is a 4 m (13 ft.) falls, easily portaged or lined on river right. Just below Fourth Pond, there is a series of small ledges followed by a narrow chute which is usually too narrow and rocky to run. You can haul around it on the right.

WATER NOTES: The high waters of April or May are best for this trip. Low water means dragging your boat for considerable distances between ponds.

DISTANCE: 30 km (19 mi.).

DURATION: 2-3 days.

DESCRIPTION: This is a good trip for novice boaters who want to get a feel for the wilderness, but do not want to get in over their heads. Most of this river can be and at times has to be waded. However, the stream is pretty and the experience can be enjoyable. In Newfoundland, most bodies of water are called "ponds" and not lakes, as in most other parts of the country. At which point a pond becomes a lake eludes us and we have yet to get an answer to the question. Since some of the "ponds" in Newfoundland are more than 20 km (12 mi.) long and some of the lakes are less than 1 km (0.6 mi.), we would suspect it has nothing to do with size.

The first 8 ponds are connected by very short sections of river which can be paddled in high water or lined and waded in low. Low relief coupled with long arms make finding the outlet of some of these ponds difficult. Follow your map carefully. The next stretch is a little over a kilometre of meandering stream which at times requires wading and hauling over fallen trees and the occasional beaver dam. Two more small ponds with short sections of river bring you to Fourth Pond, a good place for brook trout. Below Fourth Pond the river picks up in both speed and volume. There are several ledges which usually have to be lined or hauled around. The next 2 km (1.2 mi.) are swift current except for a small ledge just before Ripple Pond. Campsites here are numerous and beautiful along the grassy banks of the river. From Ripple Pond to Colinet is a delightful run down swift water with the occasional Class 2 thrown in for fun. The trip ends near the ocean at the community of Colinet.

LOGISTICS: Turn off the Ocean Pond access road from the Trans Canada Highway 60 km (37 mi.) west of St. John's. Drive 2.4 km (1.5 mi.) and turn left onto the Fox Marsh access road. Follow this for another 3.8 km (2.5 mi.) and the pond on your right is the put-in.

MAPS: 1N/4-1N/6.

CHART: N/A.

Middle Three Island Pond

RAPIDS: N/A.

WATER NOTES: A series of small ponds.

DISTANCE: 3-15 km (2-9 mi.).

DURATION: 2-10 hours.

DESCRIPTION: An enjoyable day trip only 20 minutes from the capital city of St. John's, it begins at Middle Three Island Pond which has a diverse and interesting shoreline containing the 3 islands plus 2 long fjord-like arms. Since herring gulls nest on the small island in the centre of the pond, keep a reasonable distance from the island during their nesting season.

After Middle Three Island Pond are Middle, Moon, and Half Moon Ponds. The further you go, the more remote the feeling and the smaller the ponds. The untouched forest and the unspoiled waters of Moon Pond carry this remote sensation even though it is only 20 minutes from St. John's.

There is talk of ghosts on these waterways, so do not be surprised as you paddle in the fog if you hear church bells toll (from Torbay, 10 km away) or an organ play in the forest you cannot see. Trouting has traditionally been good in this area—prize-size rainbow trout up to 4.5 kg (10 lbs.) make this a good but challenging place to fish. If you are looking for an evening paddle or an all day affair close to St. John's, this is a great option.

LOGISTICS: The put-in for this trip is at the boat launch off Three Island Pond Road. Take Torbay Road (Route 20) out of St. John's and then the Bauline Line (Route 21). Three Island Pond Road is opposite the softball field. As you go down the dirt road you will come to a gravel pit and a fork in the road. Take the right fork. Continue on about 300 m (984 ft.) and you will find the boat launch on your left.

It is possible to take-out at Middle Pond, but the car shuttle would take 5 times longer than the short paddle and portage back to the put-in at Middle Three Island Pond.

MAP: 1N/10.

CHARTS: N/A.

Rocky River

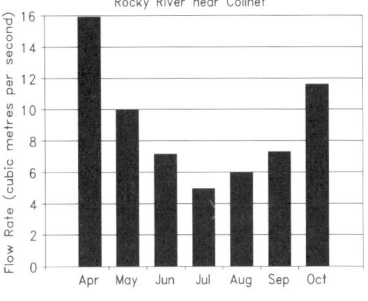
Rocky River near Colinet

RAPIDS: Class 1.

WATER NOTES: Moving water with a falls just after the egress.

DISTANCE: 15 km (9 mi.).

DURATION: 2-5 hours.

DESCRIPTION: Best paddled after heavy rain or runoff, the Rocky is an easy, quiet and meandering river ideally suited to both the novice and the avid paddler. Grassy riverbanks are common and make ideal lunch or rest stops.

This is a good river to paddle at the beginning of the paddling season as a warm up to the more vigorous and challenging trips later in the season.

LOGISTICS: At Whitbourne Junction, go south 8 km (5 mi.) on Route 81 to Markland. The put-in is the Hodge River tributary at the bridge just before the church on the right. The egress for the trip is where Rocky River crosses Route 91. Since there is a nasty drop just above the bridge, be sure to get off the river on the left side as soon as the bridge becomes visible. As Routes 81 and 91 are dirt roads, travelling along them may be slow.

MAPS: 1N/4, 1N/5.

CHART: N/A.

Soloing on a quiet stretch of river.

Petty Harbour to Bay Bulls

RAPIDS: N/A, ocean paddling.

WATER NOTES: The entire length of this trip is totally exposed to the North Atlantic. Even moderate onshore winds can cause major swells to rebound off cliff faces resulting in chaotic conditions near the shore. This, coupled with the lack of landing zones, makes the trip suitable only for experienced boaters who have checked the sea conditions and weather forecast before proceeding.

DISTANCE: 28 km (17 mi.).

DURATION: 1 long day.

DESCRIPTION: The trip can be paddled in either direction, but because of the prevailing south and southwest winds it is normally best to travel north from Bay Bulls. The first 5 km (3 mi.) are fairly sheltered, giving you a chance to build up gradually to the feel of the open ocean. Once around the navigational light at Bull Head all signs of habitation disappear and for the next 18 km (11 mi.) there are only 2 or 3 places where you can go ashore safely. Seven kilometres (4.3 mi.) of paddling along craggy cliffs and innumerable nooks and crannies will bring you to the "Spout," the start of a 4 km (2.5 mi.) spectacular paddle which local kayakers refer to as a "Disney World" for sea kayakers. This 4 km (2.5 mi.) stretch is filled with many surprises including caves, sea stacks, waterfalls and of course "The Spout." This natural phenomena is produced by a sea cave and a small freshwater brook running in through a vertical shaft into the top of the cave. Wave action into the cave can force spray up through this shaft more than 10 m (33 ft.) into the air. Nearby, there is a boulder beach which provides a landing spot when conditions permit. Good footwear, however, and possibly a rope, are needed to access the spout.

Three kilometres (1.8 mi.) past the spout is Shoal Bay, one of the few reasonable take-out points along the trip. The trail from Shoal Bay to the Southern Shore Highway (Route 10) is approximately 7 km (4.3 mi.) long and affords an emergency exit if required. From here to Petty Harbour, there are no more landing zones. The landscape remains severe and spectacular with exposed bedrock and very little vegetation. Great caution should be exercised when rounding Motion Head, the most easterly point of the trip, where numerous overfalls can cause violent seas in heavy swell situations. The trip ends in Petty Harbour, which is protected by breakwaters and is the site where the movie *Orca* was filmed.

LOGISTICS: The put-in is at the community slipway in Bay Bulls, 30 km (19 mi.) south of St. John's on Route 10. Take-out is at a wooden slipway on the north side of Petty Harbour, which is accessed by following Route 10 to the community of Goulds and turning left on Petty Harbour Road.

MAP: 1N/7.

CHART: 4845.

Salmonier Line - Middle Gull Pond - Brigus Junction

RAPIDS: N/A, flat water.

WATER NOTES: A series of small ponds with the possibility of large lakes, depending on the chosen route.

DISTANCE: 1-50 km (1-31 mi.).

DURATION: 1 hour-5 days.

DESCRIPTION: The Avalon Peninsula consists of primarily boreal forest and maritime barrens. Any trip in this area will include portage after portage as you hop from gulley to gulley or pond to pond. As you portage over the bogs, watch out for the "black holes" (bogs) that await, ready to suck the boots off the unsuspecting person carrying a pack or canoe.

Since there are endless possible routes, it is best to select one route beforehand, but leave it open to possible modification. The common start or finish points include: Brigus Junction, Middle Gull Pond and Hawcos Pond. Trouting is generally good, and wildlife is fairly abundant throughout the more remote regions.

This trip is often done by new paddlers looking for a canoe trip. Since many landmarks look alike in this area, map and compass skills are highly recommended.

LOGISTICS: For Middle Gull Pond and Brigus Junction, take the respective turnoff from the Trans Canada Highway. To access Hawcos Pond, take the Salmonier Line, Route 90 off the Trans Canada Highway approximately 9.3 km (5.7 mi.). You will come to Deer Park Road on your right. Follow that about 5 km (3 mi.) to Hawcos Pond. There are many cabins in this area; check with the locals for more details.

MAPS: 1N/3, 1N/6.

CHART: N/A.

Typical rock shoreline.

Salmonier River

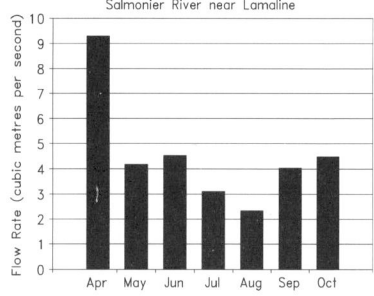

Salmonier River near Lamaline

RAPIDS: Riffles are along the river and one tidal rapid is under the bridge at the end. If play boating is your interest, skip the trip and go to the tidal rapid at high water and low tide.

WATER NOTES: Should be run at high water. Beware of sweepers at blind turns, especially after flooding. The rapid under the bridge at the egress is tidal and may change significantly in the time it takes to run the river.

DISTANCE: 14 km (9 mi.).

DURATION: 3-6 hours.

DESCRIPTION: This river is only paddlable with snow melt or rain run-off. Otherwise, it becomes a "drag." This is an easy trip to do with a novice paddler as the only things to watch for are possible sweepers and the tidal rapid at the mouth of the river. The river snakes its way along through heavily forested valley and roughly parallel to the road until it reaches an area called the flats. Here, it meanders through grass and marsh, providing a pleasant contrast to the first part of the trip. Although the current is moving, there are no significant rapids, though there will be the occasional rock to avoid or small surfing wave to hog. For the experienced river paddler, the most interesting parts of this trip will be the comaraderie, salmon fishing and the tidal rapid (if the tide is out). The tidal rapid can be an enjoyable play spot for open boat or kayak.

LOGISTICS: Paddlers can reach the Salmonier River by taking the Salmonier Line (Route 90) until you come to the turn off for "River Run Resort" (this name is subject to change) and follow the signs. About 100 m (330 ft.) behind the main complex you will find the put-in. Locals refer to that part of the river as Governors Falls.

A car can be left near the bridge where Route 90 crosses the river while you are paddling. This also gives you the opportunity to have a look at the tidal rapid there.

MAP: 1N/3.

CHART: N/A.

Kevin Redmond

Family outing on Salmonier River.

Kevin Redmond

South Coast of Newfoundland.

Kevin Redmond

Sandbanks, South Coast.

Mark Dykeman

Single family left after resettlement.

Kevin Redmond

A Humpback's tail, East Coast.

Dan Murphy

Terra Nova National Park.

Kevin Redmond

Bay of Islands, West Coast.

Kevin Redmond

Bay du Nord aerial.

Kevin Redmond

Near Cape St. Mary's.

Kevin Redmond

Newman Sound.

Jim Price

Spring paddling near Flatrock: 15 minutes drive from St. John's.

Kevin Redmond

Two-hundred foot cave in Middle Cove.

Holyrood Pond

RAPIDS: N/A, flat water.

WATER NOTES: Even though this is a pond, the south end runs into the ocean and, therefore, contains a significant proportion of salt water.

DISTANCE: 1-50 km (1-31 mi.).

DURATION: 1 hour-2 days.

DESCRIPTION: Holyrood Pond has the unique feature of being connected to the ocean. As a result, it is possible to experience both salt and freshwater animal and plant life. It is not uncommon, for example, to encounter otters.

Deer River flows into Holyrood Pond like a water slide with a 30 m (100 ft.) vertical drop. With the eastern-shoreline boasting cliffs of 150 m (500 ft.), it makes for a spectacular backdrop to an enjoyable paddle.

If you are interested in a wilderness campsite, you can camp at the north end of the lake and paddle back the second day. If you are looking for convenience, there is a provincial park on the western side of Holyrood Pond. In our case, we made a poor choice of site. It happened to be in the middle of a moose trail. It was one of those times when you would like to see a moose but not so close that you could smell his breath as we did early the following morning.

LOGISTICS: Take Route 90 (Salmonier Line) south approximately 75 km (47 mi.) to St. Vincents. Holyrood Pond is about 1 km (0.5 mi.) past the community on your left.

MAPS: 1K/13, 1K/14.

CHART: N/A.

Deer River water slide flowing into Holyrood Pond.

Lower Lance Cove - Ireland's Eye Loop

RAPIDS: N/A, ocean paddling.

WATER NOTES: Tides or tidal currents are not a problem here. The area is relatively well sheltered; however, an easterly wind can present problems, especially when paddling out.

DISTANCE: 45-80 km (29-50 mi.) depending on what option you choose.

DURATION: 2-4 days.

DESCRIPTION: Random Island, located on the north side of Trinity Bay, is 35 km (22 mi.) long and is the largest island off the coast of Newfoundland. One half of its area is covered with fresh water, forming a myriad of ponds, gullies and streams— a delight to the fishing enthusiast. This unique island is separated from the mainland by river-like passages, giving it the appearance of a fjord.

Out of the 27 communities originally settled on Random Island, only 12 remain, some with populations as low as 30 inhabitants.

The trip starts on a quiet beach in Lower Lance Cove. As you paddle east, the towering cliffs are a prime nesting area for the majestic bald eagle. You should see several of these magnificent creatures as you explore this rugged coast. Three or 4 hours of steady paddling will bring you to the abandoned community of Thoroughfare. This once-thriving fishing and logging community was one of the earliest settlements and existed for more than 130 years until a government program resettled them in the 1960s. Evidence of this long-abandoned community still lingers, and the tranquil meadow-like setting makes for an ideal campsite.

While investigating the remains of this once-flourishing community, you will notice the trees and shrubs slowly covering over the relics of man as the area returns to nature. You can also see graveyards and tombstones of the early settlers as you follow the remnants of the old road around the community. From this base camp, you can circumnavigate Ireland's Eye Island just off shore and paddle on to British Harbour, complete with its resident population of Newfoundland ponies, or meander southward and sail around Random Island itself. All these options are equally rewarding.

LOGISTICS: Leave the Trans Canada Highway at Clarenville on Route 230. Turn right on Route 231 to Random Island and take the next left to Britannia. Continue on to Lower Lance Cove which is at the end of the road.

MAPS: 2C/3, 2C4.

CHART: 4852.

Ireland's Eye.

Mark Dykeman

RAPIDS: N/A, ocean paddling.

WATER NOTES: This area is exposed to the North Atlantic. Because of the shortage of landing zones, check weather and wind forecasts before setting out.

DISTANCE: 13 km (8 mi.).

DURATION: 4-5 hours.

DESCRIPTION: The "dragon's throat" is a cave on the north end of Great Island, 1 of 4 islands which make up the Witless Bay Ecological Reserve. This cave is more than 100 m deep and narrows to only a few metres, allowing restricted access to the cavern inside. After judging the sea conditions, we ducked our heads and darted our kayaks inside the black hall of the inner chamber. The roar of the water breaking on a gravel beach somewhere in the black back of the cave made us feel uneasy, so after a few hasty sweeps of our paddles we could see light beaming through the narrow passage we had just come through. A couple of forward strokes and we were back out in the larger expanses of the main cave. One of the other members in the group asked if she could go in and have a look around. We shook our heads saying that the swells coming in were unpredictable, and it would not be wise for a novice to enter the inner cave. Then, as if on cue, a huge swell passed under us and turned the inner chamber into a seething mess of white froth and foam. "See what we mean," we said, and paddled on out of the cave.

This trip begins in the small fishing village of Bauline East and heads directly east towards Great Island, one of the best breeding grounds for seabirds in the world. During the peak nesting period, as many as 2 or 3 million birds inhabit this tiny island, making for a spectacular aerial show.

From Great Island, you can head southwest toward the abandoned community of La Manche which was devastated by a great tidal wave in 1966.

Sea stack and seabirds, Great Island.

Jim Price

Residents finally abandoned the community and left it to the mercy of the sea. The grass meadows among the remains of the old concrete foundations make for a great lunch spot. La Manche is now part of a Provincial Park and the trail behind the community leads along the La Manche River toward camping facilities accessible from the Southern Shore Highway. A short 4 km (2.5 mi.) paddle along the cliffs and headlands brings you back to Bauline East. Common along this coast are sightings of whales and, in early summer, giant icebergs.

LOGISTICS: From St. John's, travel south on Route 10 to the small community of Tors Cove. Just past the community, turn left at the sign "St. Michael's." Drive to the end of the road and there is a slipway where you can launch your boats.

MAP: 1N/2.

CHART: 4845.

Reflections: Witless Bay Ecological Reserve

Newfoundland and Labrador has one of the largest concentrations of seabirds in the world. Every year, millions of seabirds leave the open oceans and inhabit the reserve. Here, in 1 of the province's 6 seabird ecological reserves, over 1.1 million pairs of seabirds gather to breed during the summer months.

Located between the communities of Bay Bulls and Bauline on the coast of the historic Southern Avalon, the Witless Bay Ecological Reserve is comprised of 4 islands: Great, Green, Gull and Pee Pee Islands which have a 1 km marine boundary surrounding them.

A visit to the Reserve is a breathtaking encounter with a multitude of seabird species. The second largest Common Murr colony and the largest Atlantic Puffin colony in North America, Witless Bay is also the second largest Leach's Storm-Petrel colony in the world.

During the caplin run from about mid-June to mid-July, seabirds are most active. Joined by fisherman and whales in pursuit of this favorite fish, this is an exciting time to visit the Reserve and marvel at the abundance of wildlife under the sea, in the air and on the land.

Although the islands are too sensitive to tolerate human presence, local tour boat and sea kayak operators offer a thrilling tour around the islands where you see many of the seabird species and quite possibly whales and icebergs.

— Condensed from "Witless Bay Islands Seabird
Ecological Reserve Management Plan," a Parks
and Natural Areas Division publication.

Central Newfoundland

Ragged Harbour River.

> In the west, to our expressible delight, the interior broke in sublimity before us. What a contrast did this present to the conjectures entertained of Newfoundland! The hitherto mysterious interior lay unfolded below us, a boundless scene, an emerald surface, a vast basin. The eye strides again and again over a succession of northerly and southerly ranges of green plains, marbled with woods and lakes of every form and extent, a picture of all the luxurious scenes of national cultivation, receding in invisibleness. The imagination hovers in the distance, and clings involuntarily to the undulating horizon of vapour, far into the west, until lost. A new world seemed to invite us onwards, or rather we claimed the dominion and were impatient to proceed to take possession.
>
> —W.E. Cormack, *Narrative of a Journey*
> *Across the Island of Newfoundland in 1822*

The central region of the province includes the area west of Terra Nova National Park to Springdale in the north and Burgeo in the south. This region lies within the boundaries of three ecoregions: Maritime barrens, north shore forests and central Newfoundland forests. The coastal regions along the north are interrupted by many deep bays and inlets. In the south, the land takes on a rolling appearance dominated by balsam and spruce forests. Still further south, the land becomes barren with many bogs, with forests found only in sheltered valleys. The summer temperatures vary considerably with the warmest coastal regions in the province to the north, through to warm summers inland and cooler along the southern portions.

This region has its own rich history. It is the land of the long lost "Red Indian" or Beothuck who travelled inland along the Exploits River in search of caribou and to the Bay of Exploits to fish salmon. At one time, the Beothucks could be found living over most parts of the island, but constant pressures from European settlers eventually forced them to retreat inland along the shore of the Exploits River and Red Indian Lake.

The coastal areas are dotted with fishing communities protected from the North Atlantic by hundreds of bays and inlets. Some of these communities have a history as old as the fishing industry itself.

Central

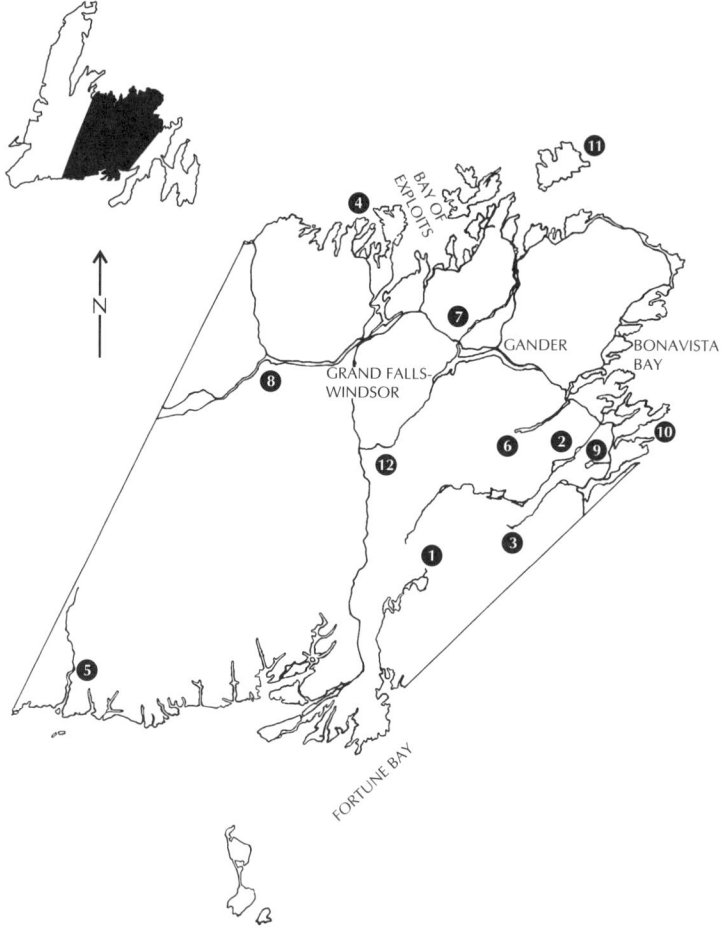

1 Bay Du Nord River
2 Terra Nova River
3 Northwest River
4 Notre Dame River
5 White Bear River
6 Gambo Pond
7 Lower Gander River

8 Exploits River
9 Sandy Pond to Terra Nova Lake
10 Terra Nova National Park
   (Newman Sound)
11 Fogo Island
12 Northwest Gander River

Bay du Nord River

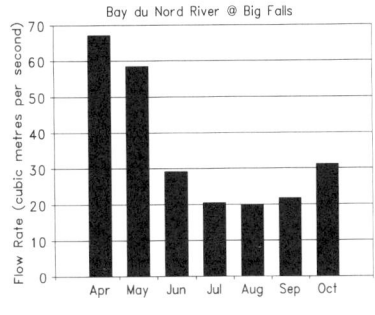

Bay du Nord River @ Big Falls

RAPIDS: Class 2-3 with the occasional Class 4 and 5. Portaging and lining are relatively easy around unrunnable sections except for Smokey Falls and the section above Jubilee Lake which requires bushwacking around the left side.

WATER NOTES: One of the toughest sections is the last 0.5 km before Jubilee Lake. A series of waterfalls ranging from 2-3 m (7-10 ft.) makes this area unrunnable except for experts in closed boats.

DISTANCE: 75 km (47 mi.) (from Diamond Lake).

DURATION: 5-7 days.

DESCRIPTION: This 2,895 km² (1,117 mi.²) of Newfoundland's southeastern interior with its roadless wilderness is a haven for large populations of caribou, moose and Canada geese, as well as brook trout and landlocked salmon. The Bay du Nord River has been nominated as a Canadian Heritage River.

Declared a Wilderness Reserve in 1990, the undisturbed, picturesque waterway of the Bay du Nord and its chain of headwaters lakes offers a relatively short but exhilarating true wilderness canoe adventure.

The first half of the canoe trip combines a series of beautiful lakes intermixed with short stretches of river. From Diamond Lake, it is an easy 30-minute hike to the top of Mount Sylvester, the highest point in the area. Rapids ranging from class 2 to 3 are common in the short sections between the lakes and some lining and portaging is necessary to negotiate the more difficult drops.

After crossing Medonnegonix Lake, a micmac Indian name for "End of Portage," the river starts its descent in earnest. As it crashes its way to the sea, it runs through

Smokey Falls.

Department of Natural Resources, Wildlife Division

rock gorges and plunges over several falls, including the magnificent Smokey Falls, over 30 m (100 ft.) high. Flat water sections or "steadies" are welcome sights where you can take it easy or do some fishing. There are many stretches of runnable white water here but some portaging and lining is required.

The river's character changes dramatically as it approaches the sea. The valley widens and the surroundings take on a fjord-like appearance. The last waterfall lures salmon fishermen to try their luck for the prized Atlantic salmon which migrate up at least as far as Smokey Falls. At the mouth of the river, you will find the remnants of the abandoned fishing village Bay du Nord, victim of a government resettlement programme of the early 1960s. From here, there is a 4 km (2.5 mi.) open water paddle across North Bay to the colourful outport of Pool's Cove.

LOGISTICS: This trip can be accessed by float plane at any of the large lakes which comprise the Bay du Nord system. A favourite starting point is Diamond Lake. This gives one the opportunity to hike Mt. Sylvester before lining and hauling down a small creek several hundred yards to one of the main tributaries.

The take-out is at Pool's Cove. From here, if you have a vehicle, you can drive north 160 km (100 mi.) on the Bay d' Espoir Highway, Route 360, to the Trans Canada Highway. For a more adventurous ending to this trip, you can catch the southcoast ferry from English Harbour West for a reasonable rate. This passes some of the most spectacular coastal scenery in Newfoundland and docks at Terrenceville, 2.5 hours from St. John's by car.

MAPS: 2D/3, 1M/11, 1M/14.

CHART: N/A.

Reflections: The Atlantic Salmon

Do not be alarmed by a sudden splash in the middle of the night, a flash of silver just off the bow of your canoe or a mighty fish leaping skyward as you paddle through a quiet pool. What you have seen or heard is most likely the Atlantic salmon which inhabits many of the larger rivers of Newfoundland and Labrador.

Kevin Redmond

Prized by anglers, the Atlantic salmon symbolizes true wilderness and wildness. The life cycle of the Atlantic salmon is a mystery in its own right. Depending on the river, the spawning run will begin sometime between May and November, with spawning occurring in the fall. Thousands of eggs are deposited by each female. After wintering in the gravel and being washed by cool clear waters, the eggs will hatch in the spring. Young salmon may spend from 2-6 years in the fresh water until, like their parents, they return to the sea for up to 3 years. Then, as if called by mother nature herself, they will begin a long swim home to the river of their birth to spawn, ensuring that one of nature's most mysterious cycles will repeat itself.

Terra Nova River

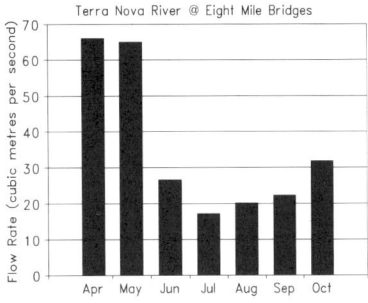

Terra Nova River @ Eight Mile Bridges

RAPIDS: Sections 1 and 2 have rapids ranging from Class 1 to 3, with a couple of Class 4 ledges at high water. Section 3 has mostly Class 3 and 4 except at high water when Class 5 and 6 can be encountered. Careful scouting is recommended.

WATER NOTES: Extreme caution is advised when approaching the 15 m (50 ft.) waterfall at the salmon ladder below Terra Nova Lake.

DISTANCE: ○ Section 1 - 30 km (19 mi.);
○ Section 2 - 70 km (44 mi.);
○ Section 3 - 23 km (14 mi.).

DURATION: ○ Section 1 - 2 days;
○ Section 2 - 3-4 days;
○ Section 3 - 1-2 days.

DESCRIPTION: The Terra Nova is one of the most enjoyable yet most challenging rivers in Newfoundland. Each section has a different appeal, from the wilderness experience of the first section to the thrills of white water madness on the last. Several Atlantic Salmon enhancement projects also add to the diversity of this charming river.

If you fly into the head waters and paddle the first section, you will undoubtedly be confronted with numerous wildlife sightings—moose, caribou, black bears, Canada Geese and ducks, just to name a few of the common sightings. Several short portages may be required around small ledges and at low water; wading your canoe through boulder gardens is the order of the day.

Beginning at the outlet of Lake St. John, known locally as John's Pond, the character of the river changes. Calm steadies are interspersed with short, enjoyable rapids. Mollyguajeck Falls is the only major obstacle in this section and can be easily portaged on the north side.

The last section of the Terra Nova is the most challenging for both open and closed boats alike. Several Class 4-5 rapids along with a 5 m (16.4 ft.) runnable waterfall is plenty to get the adrenaline flowing in most of us. Portaging for the most part is easy and many of the rapids can be lined.

LOGISTICS: Section 1, starting at the head water lake, is accessed by float plane only. Section 2 is accessed either by float plane to Lake St. John or by a very rough woods road leading from the Village of Terra Nova. A 4-wheel drive is recommended. Section 3 can be accessed by car at the Village of Terra Nova. The take-out is at Spencer's Bridge on the Trans Canada Highway.

MAPS: 2D/6, 2D/7, 2D/8, 2D/9.

CHART: N/A.

Northwest River

RAPIDS: Most are easy, Class 1 and 2 rapids.

WATER NOTES: Plastic boats and a cheerful disposition are a must when negotiating the shin-bruising boulder gardens.

DISTANCE: ○ Meta Pond to Northwest Pond - 78 km (48 mi.);

○ Endless Lake to Northwest Pond - 55 km (31 mi.);

○ Ninety-Nine Island Pond to Northwest Pond - 40 km (25 mi.).

DURATION: ○ Meta Pond to Northwest Pond - 5 days;

○ Endless Lake to Northwest Pond - 3 days;

○ Ninety-Nine Island Pond to Northwest pond - 2 days.

DESCRIPTION: Northwest River drains a large number of adjoining lakes in the central portion of the Bay du Nord Wilderness Area. Overall, at moderate to high water levels, it offers an enjoyable and modestly challenging canoe experience.

If the river does not set your spirits on high, the wildlife sightings most certainly will. On our first trip down this river (when one of us worked with the Department of Forestry), we were accused of having Forestry staff release animals on the shores of the river to impress fellow canoeists. This, of course, was not the case and we were equally impressed with the numerous animals roaming quite casually along the river bank as if just stepping from Noah's ark. Such sightings include moose, caribou, bear, beaver, otter, Canada geese, nesting osprey, loons, several species of ducks, red squirrels and a wide variety of songbirds.

The trip from Meta Pond requires 9 short portages over mainly barren land to access the headwaters of the Northwest River. Here, the river is small and passes through several connecting steadies which frequently require wading and short carries. Many large white pine trees holding the occasional osprey nest and shading beautiful fishing pools dot the shoreline.

Below Ninety-Nine Island Pond, the character of the river changes to more open, better drained shores with birch glades and frequent pleasant campsites. This improvement continues, enabling evening hikes to the beckoning bare ridges above camp for a spectacular view of the valley. Most of the rapids in this section are pleasantly runnable with a few requiring scouting, lining and 1 or 2 short portages. The trip ends at Northwest Pond, a pretty body of water with several sandy beaches and a Boy Scout Camp on the eastern shore.

LOGISTICS: Access to all starting points is by float plane only. Because of the rock-studded nature of Ninety-Nine Island Pond, many pilots will not land. Check with your air charter before finalizing your plans. Egress: Northwest Pond is connected by a short stretch of road to the Trans Canada Highway just east of Terra Nova National Park.

MAPS: 2D/2, 2D/7, 2D/8.

CHART: N/A.

Notre Dame Bay

RAPIDS: N/A, ocean paddling.

WATER NOTES: As in most areas around Newfoundland, tides in Notre Dame Bay present no problems to the sea kayaker. Carry ample drinking water with you if you do not know where to find it.

DISTANCE: 2-200 km (1-125 mi.).

DURATION: Trips in the Notre Dame Bay area can range from a 2-hour paddle around Gander Island to a 10-day excursion around Twillingate, Fogo and New World Island.

DESCRIPTION: Newfoundland's coastline is exposed to the North Atlantic. This area, however, is a welcomed relief, especially for the novice sea kayaker. A real gem for sea kayaking, it is located on the northwest coast and boasts of thousands of islands just begging to be explored. You can spend literally weeks here exploring the many stunning bays, coves, runs and arms and never have to venture out onto the open ocean.

One of the best ways to see this area is to do some "causeway kayaking"—that is, put in at a causeway, circumnavigate an island and return to your vehicle or camp site. Twillingate, New World and Chapel Islands can all be paddled in this way, although some may require multiple day trips. The northern ends of some of the larger islands could get rough because of rebound waves from the tall bluffs with no buffer from the Atlantic. Caution is advised.

Stunted spruce and balsam fir cover many of the smaller uninhabited islands as a result of exposure to wind and harsh weather. This low relief appearance makes them look smaller than they really are. In fact, many are quite large but almost never more than a 5-minute paddle from one to another. The whole effect is one of intimacy and, because of their inviting nature, you will find yourself drawn to them like a magnet.

The western end of Notre Dame Bay is a little more rugged and spectacular. The rock formations change giving many caves, arches and sea stacks—a delight for the more adventurous. Care should be taken when entering any cave. If a cave were to fill up with you in it, the upward force between your boat and the top of the cave could be more than 500 kg (1,100 lbs.)—enough to make you a lot shorter than you ever wanted to be.

LOGISTICS: Notre Dame Bay can be accessed by a multitude of side roads exiting the Trans Canada Highway at various locations. Travelling east from St. John's, the first is Route 320 at Gambo. Route 330 exits at Gander and Route 340, the shortest, leaves the Trans Canada Highway at Notre Dame Junction. Route 350 gives you access to the Bay of Exploits area while Routes 380, 390 and 391 will get you to western Notre Dame Bay.

MAPS: 2E/1-2E/12.

CHART: 4520 (more detailed charts available for specific areas. Use chart 4520 as index).

White Bear River

RAPIDS: The upper and lower sections range from Class 1-3; the middle canyon section ranges from Class 4-6.

WATER NOTES: This is a trip for experienced paddlers in closed boats. Expert open canoeists with a fully outfitted boat and a good roll will find it very challenging. The difficult rapids occur in a 5 km (3 mi.) section of the canyon. Most are easily portaged, but a few require a strenuous climb down exposed bedrock. A seal entry was required to re-enter the river on several locations in this section. Many of the falls are runnable, especially in low water.

DISTANCE: White Bear Lake to Ramea - 77 km (49 mi.).

DURATION: 3-4 days.

DESCRIPTION: In a *Canoe* article entitled "The 10 best paddlers in North America," Tom McKewin, a 25 year veteran paddler, described a trip on the White Bear as the most memorable kayak trip he had ever been on. Since he had world wide paddling experience, this kind of testimony did not go unnoticed. Several years later, another group arrived on the scene from the U.S. and made the second run of this great river. It was not until 1993 that Newfoundland's "crack boaters" or "crackpot boaters" decided to literally take the plunge and run the White Bear.

We were really up for the trip until Jamie, one of the crack team, told us of his dream, or should we say nightmare. Apparently, our tent was pitched on a narrow crag several hundred metres above the river. To the left, was a 3 m (11 ft.) tall polar bear, rearing up on its hind legs and moving menacingly toward the tent. To the right, was an equally large grizzly also closing in on the lone occupant—Jamie. With his back to the rock wall, he knew there was only one escape. He charged through the open door of the tent and leapt off the cliff toward the river below. Falling, falling, the river zoomed up at him with ever increasing speed. He braced his body to take the shock of impact when suddenly—he woke up, drenched not in river water, but sweat.

Well, this drama was not played out on the river, but we did have our bear encounter. About 0.5 km down river from White Bear Lake, a huge black bear crossed the river less than 100 m (300 ft.) in front of us. As it waded to the right, we took the "chicken route" to the left and we pointed to the bear to alert Jamie. Farther down river, we laughed and asked Jamie if the bear was as big as the one in his dream. "What bear?" he replied. Apparently, he had thought we were pointing to the best route through the shallow rapids and did not even see the animal cross right in front of us.

Much of the White Bear's energy has been robbed by hydro development, which has diverted the water into the Bay d' Espoir system. This has caused the first section of the river to be very shallow requiring scraping over boulder gardens, dragging boats over gravel strands and pushing oneself "gorilla-like" along the bottom. But this difficult process is a blessing in disguise, because high water in this section would mean that many of the drops in the canyon would be unrunnable. This section has several Class 3 chutes, and some more difficult ones, which deserve scouting.

The canyon section is one of the most spectacular geologic areas in the province. Sheer granite walls, innumerable waterfalls, and house-sized boulders team up to give the appearance of a gigantic Disney theme park. The most magnificent falls are those of the tributaries crashing their way through side canyons, which make for a great hiking opportunity to ease the tension of the Class 4-5 rapids. About halfway through the canyon, there is a portage around a most dastardly piece of water. The water here careens off a solid rock face to the right, turns 90°, does the same thing on river left, and so on—twice more before its energy is absorbed in the quiet pool below. An interesting highlight of this pool is a rather large cave, naturally sculptured out of the solid rock on the left side of the river. Six or 8 kayaks could easily fit inside, and you can even get out of your boat at the back of the cave and walk around.

The lower section of the river is a fun run with Class 1-3 rapids through mostly boulder gardens. When you hit White Bear Bay, you have over 30 km (19 mi.) of flat water to the take-out in Ramea. This is a relaxing paddle through a fjord-like setting lined on both sides by 300 m (980 ft.) cliffs which have dozens of water falls flowing straight into the sea.

LOGISTICS: Fly from Deer Lake airport to White Bear Lake for the put-in. The river is also accessed by driving down an old woods road past Granite Lake to Burnt Lake, but dragging your boat down the mostly dry river bed for 7 km (4 mi.) to White Bear Lake is not recommended. The coastal ferry can take you back to Terrenceville. This 12-hour cruise is well worth the money. The south coast scenery is breathtaking and Terrenceville is only 2.5 hours by car from St. John's. You can also take a coastal ferry west to Port aux Basques to link up with the Marine Atlantic ferry to mainland Canada.

MAPS: 12A/3, 11P/14, 11P/11.

CHART: (for coastal portion of trip) 4663.

Cave Rapid, White Bear River.

Gambo Pond

RAPIDS: Class 1 in brook.

WATER NOTES: Flatwater, but strong east or west winds give rise to large waves. It is also possible to paddle to the salt water via Gambo Brook.

DISTANCE: 25-50 km (15-31 mi.).

DURATION: 1-3 days.

DESCRIPTION: Gambo Pond is a long, narrow pond about 25 km (15.5 mi.) in length with a prevailing westerly wind. The easier paddle is from the western end of the lake to the highway. Easterly winds are accompanied by poor weather in this region.

In recent years, the area has become more developed. The paddler's proximity to cabins provides additional safety. The pond's shoreline is dotted with sandy beaches, so camping should not be a problem. When the water is high, it is possible to run the brook from the eastern tip of the pond to the salt water, which is a couple of kilometres long with no drops or ledges—just a nice rock garden. The salmon run up the brook in season adds a pleasant diversion to the trip for the avid fisherman.

LOGISTICS: The Trans Canada Highway crosses the river at the eastern end of the pond about 0.5 km (0.3 mi.) south of the Gambo exit. If you wish to put-in directly into the pond, it is a 5-minute portage up the side of the river. This trip can even be extended by paddling the coast to the community of Gambo.

MAPS: 2D/9, 2D/10.

CHART: N/A.

Early spring paddling.

Lower Gander River

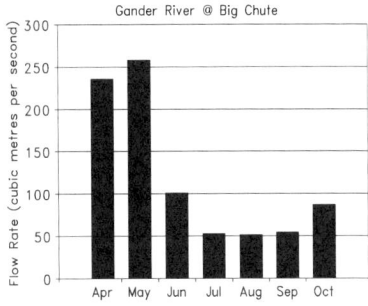

Gander River @ Big Chute

RAPIDS: Class 1-3.

WATER NOTES: Mostly flatwater paddling with short sections of river. If the water is low a minimal amount of dragging is required.

DISTANCE: 50 km (31 mi.).

DURATION: 1-3 days.

DESCRIPTION: The Lower Gander River is, for a lot of local paddlers, their first river run. This indicates its level of difficulty but, like any river, it should not be underestimated. Not far downstream from the put-in are the first 2 rapids, Little and Big Chute respectively. Both are runnable or lineable on the river right. On occasion, they are suitable for surfing. The river continues with occasional shallows, all of which have a deep water channel as you will notice as the Gander River boats go from Glenwood to Gander Bay. On one trip down the river, a 7 m (25 ft.) Gander River boat pulled into the campsite about midnight. After commenting on the ease with which people drive the boats through shallows and rapids any time of the day or night, the elderly gentleman responded, "The river is just like the highway—you just have to learn to read the signs."

There are several cabins, some private and some corporate, on the river. Most are used primarily for the salmon fishing season. Before Snake Rattle, there are 4 ponds in succession with no portages required. Winds here are generally at your back most of the time, but on occasion strong headwinds often result in a difficult paddle. Open birch lines the river, making campsites more plentiful than the dense spruce and fir forest found in the eastern region. On weekend trips, most people camp before First Pond or just above Snake Rattle: the latter is the better fishing spot.

Snake Rapid is the longest and most technical rapid on the river and the most probable place on the river that you will wrap your boat. After this enjoyable run, the current slows and the scent of the salt air becomes apparent as you approach Gander Bay.

LOGISTICS: The put-in for this trip is where the Trans Canada Highway bridge crosses over the river in Glenwood just 10 minutes' drive west of Gander. Cars can be left at the causeway in Gander Bay for the finish. Car shuttle time is approximately 2 hours, round trip.

MAPS: 2D/15, 2E/2, 2E/1, 2E/8.

CHART: N/A.

Exploits River

RAPIDS: Class 1-4, 6.

WATER NOTES: All rapids can be portaged or lined. Because the river is dam controlled, it is one of the few that can guarantee water even when the season is a dry one. Beware of floating logs and log-jams.

DISTANCE: 50 km (51 mi.).

DURATION: 2-3 days.

DESCRIPTION: Red Indian Lake and the Exploits River System (the longest river in insular Newfoundland) was the last of the traditional land of the long gone Beothuck Indians. Pressures brought on by the white settlers caused the Beothucks to retreat to central Newfoundland. It has been documented that they moved inland to Red Indian Lake in winter to hunt caribou and to the mouth of the Exploits in the summer months to fish salmon. Many archaeological sites have been found along the banks of this mighty river.

A "rapid" education is the best way to describe our first experience in what is known as "Red Indian Rattle." Since this original baptism where both canoes swamped, we have done it numerous times without incident. Big waves out in the middle of the river are for those who enjoy the big ride, while the clear run on the river left is for the cautious.

Fast current with few major obstacles makes this trip generally a relaxing ride. For those who like to play, there are several places to spend an afternoon river surfing.

Approximately 32 km (20 mi.) downstream from the dam is Red Indian Falls. The left side is the better portage route. The only reasonable campsite is on the river right at the falls. Here, it is possible to view the falls and decide what route you would take if you were to run it.

Solo on the Exploits River.

Canyons, Coves and Coastal Waters

Kevin Redmond

"Dogging" the Colinet River.

Bill Band

Keeping a respectable distance from the breakers near Bauline East, Southern Shore.

Mark Dykeman

The view from Dragon's Throat Cave on Great Island.

Bill Band

Spring ice in Conception Bay.

Jim Price

Near Petty Harbour on Dick Wheeler's EPHOC, 1,500 mile South Coast Great Auk Expedition.

Harry Butt

"The Stopper," Bay du Nord.

Mark Gerin

Approaching Stuart's Staircase, Terra Nova River.

Punching through "The Rooster Tail" on the Terra Nova River.

Do not drink the water below the community of Badger since many communities empty their sewage directly into the river. There are several small rapids which lead up to "The Steps and the Badger Chute." If in doubt, keep to river left. If you wish to run the steps and chute they should be scouted first. Because it is a dam controlled river, water levels can change from day to day and these rapids can be Class 3 or 4 depending on the day or where you decide to run them. Below the chute on the river right are a couple of enjoyable play holes—a good place to spend a few hours.

A strong current coupled with birch lined banks and only a few major obstacles makes the Exploits an enjoyable trip when many other rivers are too low to paddle. An added bonus is the run of the prized Atlantic salmon which migrate up this mighty river each year to spawn.

LOGISTICS: Turn off the Trans Canada Highway at Badger (Route 370 south) and go up Buchans Highway to Buchans Junction. Take the left fork for Millertown. Continue through Millertown along the south shore of Red Indian Lake until you come to the dam at the outlet of Red Indian Lake. There are several egress points for the trip. The easiest is off the Trans Canada Highway opposite Aspen Brook Provincial Day Park. A short 200 m (700 ft.) road brings you to the river's edge. If you wish, you can continue your trip and take-out in the town of Grand Falls-Windsor.

MAPS: 12A/10, 12A/15, 12A/16, 2D/13.

CHART: N/A.

Reflections: The Common Puffin

We turned our heads for a second look as a parrot flew past between us and the cliff face. "A parrot!! in Newfoundland; surely, this must be a quirk of nature," we thought. This strange bird with the highly coloured bill was none other than the common puffin, Newfoundland and Labrador's provincial bird.

Common on the east coast of this province, the puffin is often called the "sea parrot." On land, they shuffle about and at times have difficulty becoming air borne unless there is a wind. Once air borne, the puffin's flying ability compares with that of any other sea bird in its family. An excellent swimmer and diver, the puffin lives on the fish it catches as it propels itself through the water with its wings. It is not uncommon to see a puffin with 3 or 4 fish held crosswise in its bill.

Kevin Redmond

The puffin nests in colonies on coastal islands and on cliffs. Eggs are laid in a nest made at the end of a long burrow in the ground or nestled in a crack on the cliff face. The colourful beak is predominant only during the breeding season, with its bright colours fading in fall and winter. When paddling our coastal waters, be sure to keep an eye open for our "sea parrot."

Sandy Pond to Terra Nova Lake

RAPIDS: N/A.

WATER NOTES: Wind can cause large waves on Pitts Pond or Terra Nova Lake.

DISTANCE: ○ Sandy Pond to Terra Nova Lake - 25 km (15.5 mi.);

○ Sandy pond to Dunphy's Pond return - 20 km (12 mi.).

DURATION: ○ Sandy Pond to Terra Nova Lake - 2-3 days;

○ Sandy Pond to Dunphy's Pond return - 1-2 days.

DESCRIPTION: We were welcomed by blue sky, sunshine, a warm sandy beach and a light westerly wind. Eight canoes in all started from Sandy Pond paddling into the light headwind. As the pond narrowed, we found ourselves paddling a shallow stream winding through tall grasses up to 1 m (3 ft.) tall, making it difficult to catch a glimpse of a fellow paddler.

We continued through Beachy Pond and into Dunphy's Pond, where a wilderness campsite has been established at the far end of the island by Parks Canada . A warden's cabin with road access on the shore just west of the island offers a possible egress in an emergency situation. The portage to Pitts Pond is a "porkeater portage." Completing this 1 km (0.5 mi.) portage initiates you into the ranks of a true voyageur. Along the relatively clear portage trail you encounter a cut line which marks the western boundary of Terra Nova National Park.

Pitts Pond is fairly large and this makes it great for rafting up if the wind is at your back. Halfway down the pond to the right is an interesting island with a variety of nesting birds. Paddle past for a closer look, but avoid landing since it may disturb any nesting birds.

After Pitts Pond is a small stream that is entertaining for the novice with minimum risk. A final reward is the warm sandy beaches on Terra Nova Lake.

LOGISTICS: Sandy Pond to Dunphy's Pond inclusive is located in Terra Nova National Park, and visitors are required to check in at the park headquarters for appropriate permits. Campsite reservations for the Dunphy's Pond wilderness site can be made in advance by contacting park officials. See Appendix 3 for an address and telephone number.

Turn off the Trans Canada Highway in Terra Nova Park for the Sandy Pond recreational area. An approximate 25 km (15.5 mi.) car shuttle one way is required going from Sandy Pond to the Village of Terra Nova via the Trans Canada Highway and Route 111.

MAP: 2D/8.

CHART: N/A.

Terra Nova National Park (Newman Sound)

RAPIDS: N/A, ocean paddling.

WATER NOTES: Ocean conditions, exposed shores towards the mouth of the sound.

DISTANCE: 3-50 km (1-31 mi.).

DURATION: 1 hour-3 days.

DESCRIPTION: The east coast of Newfoundland is blessed with Terra Nova National Park. Established in 1957, its rich carpet of boreal forest, sparkling brooks and ponds, quiet bays and fjords beckon wilderness enthusiasts. The park boasts 200 km (124 mi.) of protected coast. Within Terra Nova National Park, Newman Sound offers a wilderness experience with the conveniences of a developed park. Putting-in at Salton's Wharf, a paddle out through "The Narrows" past the towering walls of Mount Stanford will take you into the resettled community of Minchin's Cove. This is but an appetizer for the area. Moose, bald eagles and marine life abound along its shores.

The first time we paddled the sound, it was the May 24 (Victoria Day) weekend and, sure enough, it was snowing. We had planned to go out to Swale Island but cold winds and sleet forced us into Minchin's Cove. In anticipation of a warm fire and a fine cup of tea, we failed to exercise proper caution when exiting our kayak. As we slowly sank and then bobbed in the cold waters of Newman Sound, a considerable number of appropriate incantations could be heard echoing through the forest. We did get our cup of tea, hunched over a small fire in our polypropylene underwear!

From Minchin's Cove, a hiking trail will take you to the top of Mount Stanford and offer you a breathtaking view of Newman Sound. A short paddle further up the Sound will bring you to the abandoned community of Old Broad Cove. Nestled at the end of this bay are many secret nooks and crannies to explore with your kayak.

The park offers several wilderness campsites which are excellent springboards for day-long paddles or hikes.

Despite the fact that this whole area was a thriving commercial district at the turn of the century, little evidence remains. Exploration of Minchin's Cove reveals an old dam, piers and what seems to be the remnants of old foundations, gardens and a grave site. It was during this sea kayak trip that we first realized the importance of wilderness travellers' becoming familiar with the cultural and natural history associated with their route. A little research into the area or chatting with the local park people will bring a lot more meaning and understanding to any wilderness paddling trip.

Certainly, the transition from civilization to wilderness is a tribute to the efforts of the park program in protecting and preserving some of the special places we have.

LOGISTICS: As this is a national park, appropriate permits will be required. When you check in with park officials, they will provide a park map. The turn-off for Newman Sound is off the Trans Canada Highway in the park. Launch at the boat launch at Salton's Wharf.

MAP: 2C/12.

CHARTS: British Admiralty Chart - 293; Canadian Chart - 4017.

Mount Stanford, Newman Sound.

Reflections: An Historical Review of the Resettlement Program

During the post-war period of 1945 to 1954, 49 communities were abandoned on their own initiative without Government pressure or financial assistance. It was not until 1954 that Government was requested to provide financial assistance for those undertaking such moves.

Under this pressure for financial assistance, the Government commenced a centralization program, administered by the Department of Welfare. Between 1954 and 1965, 110 communities, involving 8,000 people, were evacuated—each householder receiving somewhere between $150-$600 for moving expenses. This program was the first sign that Government intended to exert pressure on the inhabitants. The financial help was only to be given to those who were moving from a community where most of the residents had indicated their desire to resettle.

As a result of the signing of a new Federal/Provincial agreement known as The Newfoundland Fisheries Resettlement Program in 1965, further financial assistance became available. This was followed by amendments in 1967 and 1970. For the 10 year life of this Agreement, 145 designated communities were completely evacuated and 312 non-designated were partially evacuated. In all, this program involved 4,168 households and 20,656 individuals.

The rationale behind the program was to move inhabitants into larger centres where services such as health care, education and transportation were more readily available and cheaper for Government to deliver. Industrial development was to be the saviour of the province, and the fishery was to be abandoned, not only as a means of making a living, but as a way of life. The industrial age for Newfoundland, however, never did materialize and many transplanted Newfoundlanders turned bitter. They never forgave the provincial Government, led at the time by Premier Joseph R. Smallwood, for forcing them to abandon their homes and birthplaces.

Fogo Island

RAPIDS: Some streams running between ponds have fast water. These may be runnable if the water levels are high.

WATER NOTES: Winds may make paddling difficult on some of the larger ponds.

DISTANCE: Sea kayak paddle from Farewell to Man-O-War Cove is approximately 15 km (9 mi.); canoe route 11 km (7 mi.).

DURATION: 1-4 days.

DESCRIPTION: No paddling trip to the island of Newfoundland is complete without a trip to Fogo Island. The island, located off the northeast coast, provides a unique opportunity for the canoeist and sea kayaker alike to experience pristine paddling. Trout fishing is excellent in some of the less accessible ponds, so bring your fly rod.

An ideal canoe route is located on the north side of the island near the community of Tilting. The route is horseshoe shaped and takes the paddler through a series of small lakes connected by small streams, many of which can be paddled, while others require that you get out and walk. Put-in at Steady Water Pond, and paddle your way through a series of ponds. These ponds have no names, but if you study your topographic map carefully, you will see how they are all linked in a horseshoe fashion. The last leg of the trip involves a 0.5 km (0.3 mi.) drag over a peat bog. Surprisingly, the drag is quite effortless as a plastic canoe with a small load slips easily over the damp peat bog. The last time we did this section of the trip we were literally running with the canoe as we dragged it over the bog. A loud "crack" broke the silence. A fly rod, which had been laid across the top of the gear, snagged on a small tamarack and shattered into three pieces. The final leg of the trip is a short paddle down Sandy Cove Pond.

Across the road is Sandy Cove, which has one of the most beautiful sandy beaches on the island. Although there is no developed campground here, you are still welcome to pitch your tent and spend the night.

A series of hiking trails, beginning at the beach, lead to Seal Cove and Wild Cove, where you can lie in the lush green grass and look out on an emerald sea. The community of Tilting is a short walk up the road.

LOGISTICS: On Route 340 to Twillingate, take Route 331 and then 335 to Farewell. A ferry will take you across to the island located approximately 0.5 km (9 mi.), a 45 minute run. If one of your travelling partners has a sea kayak and the waters are calm and winds light, toss the kayak in and send them off. The distance between the mainland and the island can be easily paddled by following the string of islands you will see on your right. The route will take you along the Indian Islands to Man-of-War Cove where the ferry docks. The longest open water crossing is approximately 2.5 km. To begin your canoe trip, follow the signs to the small, beautiful community of Tilting. Check with the local residents for directions to Steady Water Pond and put-in there.

MAP: 2E/9.

CHART: 4531.

Northwest Gander River

RAPIDS: Class 1-3 (depending on the water level).

WATER NOTES: This river is best run in spring or heavy rain.

DISTANCE: 40-65 km (25-40 mi.).

DURATION: 2-4 days.

DESCRIPTION: We completed the car shuttle and camped at the put-in for the trip. An albino moose trotted nearby. That was a first sighting of an albino moose for the members of our party. A frosty morning greeted us. Despite the frost on the tents, it did not take long to get warmed up and going. The trip can start at Miguel's Brook, a tributary which enters the Northwest Gander River approximately 3 km (2 mi.) northwest of the Bay d'Espoir highway. Miguel's Brook is a good indicator of the water level to be expected downstream. Dragging your canoe here means a lot of dragging for the remainder of the trip.

The river meanders along through a birch and balsam forest. Aluminum canoes are not recommended for this trip since they have a tendency to stick to rocks. Even with sufficient water in the Northwest Gander, you will encounter some rocky shallows at the beginning of the trip. Do not let this deter you, however, as it can be a fantastic trip. There are 3 significant rapids on the river, the first 2 should be scouted before they are run. Lining or portaging is relatively easy if you prefer not to run them. The third rapid (Devil's Ballast Bed) is a nice boulder garden for the competent canoeist. It is unlikely that you will run the Devil's Ballast Bed the same way twice.

Bring the first exciting day of paddling to a close by making camp just below the rock garden. Moose sightings in this area are quite probable since it is a popular moose crossing. No moose crossing signs are posted, but you will find plenty of natural ones.

On the second day of the trip, there are fun runs but nothing that has to be scouted. You might find it enjoyable to raft up the river and let the current take you along. If it is not too windy, you may extend this trip by paddling to Glenwood via Gander Lake.

On many occasions, the drive to and from a canoe site can be special. Such was the case on one occasion when the return drive was on a calm, cool October night. Moonlit fog blanketed the low-lying, wooded hollows and ponds. Other ponds in higher ground glistened in the moonlight reflecting the stars above. Natural beauty like this is sure to make any drive an experience in itself.

LOGISTICS: The put-in is where the river crosses the Bay d'Espoir Highway (Route 360), approximately 70 km (47 mi.) south of the Trans Canada Highway. If you wish to paddle Gander Lake, cars can be left where the river crosses the Trans Canada Highway. To make this trip a little shorter and to avoid paddling Gander Lake, there are a couple of egress points on the woods road approximately 30 km (19 mi.) south of Glenwood. If using the latter option, check with the people in the area as to its accessibility. It is also possible to drive about 11 km (7 mi.) further up the road until you come to the steel bridge which crosses the river approximately 45 km (28 mi.) from the start of the trip.

MAPS: 2D/5, 2D/11, 2D/14.

CHART: N/A.

Jim Price

Ten Mile Pond, Gros Morne National Park.

> We then ascended for some distance up a gentle slope, and at length from the brow of a small cliff caught our first sight of Grand Pond [Grand Lake]. And a beautiful sight it was; a narrow strip of blue water, widening as it proceeded to about two miles, lay between bold rocky precipices covered with wood, and rising almost directly from the water to a height of 500 or 600 ft., having bare tops a little farther back at a still greater elevation. The pond stretched directly from us for the first six or seven miles towards the east-south-east, when it curved gradually around towards the north.
>
> — Early explorer J.B. Juke's description of Grand Lake

The west coast of Newfoundland is dominated by an ancient mountain range running approximately 450 km (278 mi.) in its length. This impressive range is an extension of the present-day Appalachian Mountains. Rising to an elevation of 822 m (2623 ft.) at their highest point, these mountain ranges provide a majestic backdrop for your canoe or kayak trip. From anywhere in western Newfoundland, it is hard to miss these old worn giants. Dusted with the first snows of winter, draped in a veil of mist or ablaze with a summer's sunset, the mountains of western Newfoundland will never cease to raise the spirit of adventure in the heart of paddler and hiker alike.

Western Newfoundland lies within four eco-regions: the Western Newfoundland Forest, the Northern Peninsula Forest, the Long Range Barrens and the Strait of Belle Isle Barrens. The climate in this region is as diverse as the land itself, with warm summers in the central and southern regions and cool, short summers in the northern regions.

Paddlers interested in the history of the land will find no shortage of it on the west coast. To the north, one will find an old Viking settlement located at L'Anse aux Meadows. Further south, ancient burial sites of the Maritime Archaic Indians are at Port au Choix. All along the coast, fishing communities with rich histories date as far back as the 1700s. The Basque whalers from Spain sailed this coast in search of whales, fish and seals, and, in 1767, Captain James Cook arrived on the west coast and charted most of its waters.

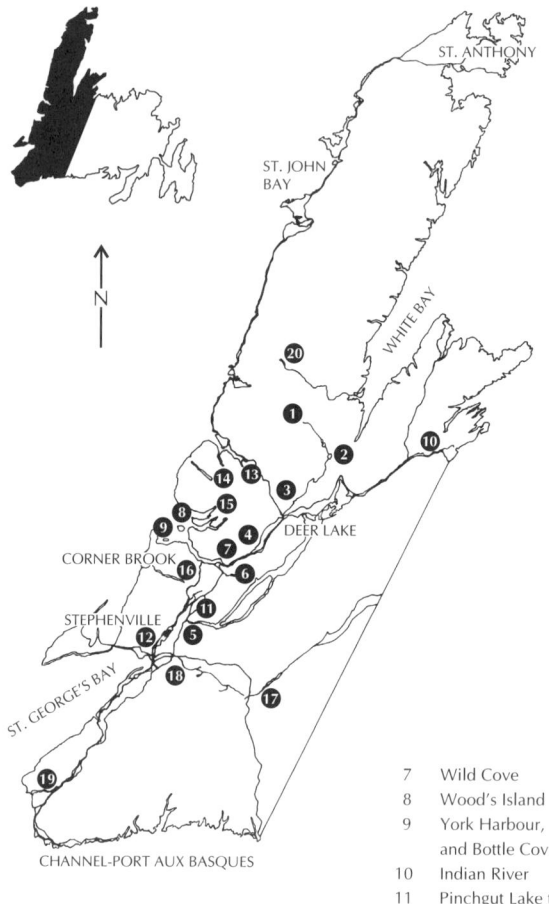

ST. ANTHONY

ST. JOHN BAY

WHITE BAY

N

20

1

2

10

14 13

3

8 15

9

7 4

DEER LAKE

16

6

CORNER BROOK

11

STEPHENVILLE

12 5

18

17

ST. GEORGE'S BAY

19

CHANNEL-PORT AUX BASQUES

1	Upper Humber River
2	Humber River (Aides Lake to Sir Richard Squires Memorial Park)
3	Humber River (Sir Richard Squires Memorial Park to Deer Lake)
4	Humber River (Deer Lake to Humber Arm)
5	Grand Lake - Sandy Lake - Birchy Lake
6	Tippens Pond (Massy Drive Pond)
7	Wild Cove
8	Wood's Island
9	York Harbour, Lark Harbour and Bottle Cove
10	Indian River
11	Pinchgut Lake to Georges Lake
12	Harrys River
13	Gros Morne National Park
14	Trout River Pond
15	North Arm, Penguin Arm and Goose Arm
16	Serpentine River
17	Lloyds River
18	Barachois Brook
19	Grand Codroy River
20	Main River

Upper Humber River

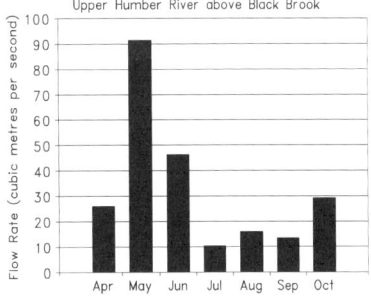

Upper Humber River above Black Brook

Due to the diversity of its character, the Humber River has been divided into 4 different routes. Each route can stand alone or the whole Humber system can be paddled as one.

RAPIDS: Many of the rapids on the upper section are long and continuous Class 3-4, especially at high water. A swim here could be a long one! Because this is a run-off river originating in the mountains, you may encounter rapid fluctuations in water levels.

WATER NOTES: The two major falls on this river have a nasty habit of sneaking up on you if you are not paying attention, so approach them with caution. The first falls is guarded with a Class 4 drop followed by 50 m (160 ft.) of easy water, giving experienced boaters the opportunity to get off the river before the major unrunnable section. The second is also guarded by a Class 4-5 drop. However, in this case, there is no time or place to get off the river before the following 15 m (50 ft.), unrunnable drop—portage both!

DISTANCE: ○ Beaver Pond to Birchy Basin - 43 km (27 mi.);

○ Silver Mountain Pond to Birchy Basin - 24 km (15 mi.).

DURATION: ○ Beaver Pond to Birchy Basin - 3-4 days;

○ Silver Mountain Pond to Birchy Basin - 1-2 days.

DESCRIPTION: Describing a river like this is one of our more enjoyable tasks. The rapids, falls and portages are all etched vividly in our minds. Pouring over maps, reviewing notes and describing the run on paper releases these mental images and lets us run the river over and over again.

Although the sound of woods trucks along the middle section of this trip detracts from its wilderness appeal, it is comforting to know that help is close at hand if an accident should occur.

Because of the diversity in the river's character, it is best described in four sections. Section 1—Beaver Pond to Silver Mountain Pond—accessible by aircraft only, bears little trace of man's influence, so canoeing this section is a superb wilderness experience. However, there is a price to pay! Water conditions are generally severe, and many sections will require lining and portaging. Section 2—the 10 km (6.25 mi.) following Silver Mountain Pond—is a fun filled roller coaster ride down continuous Class 3 rapids. One Class 4-5 rapid and an unrunable falls adds to the interest of this run. Section 3—the next 7 km (4.3 mi.)—is the easiest section of the trip. Mostly Class 1, it gives you a breather before encountering the canyon. Section 4 begins with 4 km (2.5 mi.) of rapids, with an increasing level of difficulty as you get deep into the heart of the canyon. Main Falls, a 10 m (33 ft.) drop, marks the start of the most difficult stretch. Most of the rapids are runnable; however, at high water portaging along the bank is virtually impossible. The banks are extremely steep, rising as high as 100 m (330 ft.) above the river and bearing thick vegetation. Birchy Basin starts abruptly below the mouth of the canyon and presents a striking and pleasant change to the rigorous descent just completed. A calm pool in the Basin marks the take-out and the end of the trip.

LOGISTICS: The river can be accessed at numerous locations along a major woods road paralleling its banks. If you wish, you can fly in to one of the head water lakes (Beaver Pond is a good choice) and paddle to the take-out at Birchy Basin, a total of 43 km (27 mi.). The farthest point up river accessible by road is at Silver Mountain Pond 24 km (15 mi.) from the take-out. This requires a 500 m (1600 ft.) portage from the road to the put-in. The access road leaves Route 420 approximately 28 km (17 mi.) from the Trans Canada Highway. It is in excellent condition and can be travelled easily by car.

MAPS: 12H/11, 12H/12.

CHARTS: N/A.

Bridge rapid, Upper Humber River.

Big Falls, Sir Richard Squires Memorial Park.

Humber River (Adies Lake to Sir Richard Squires Memorial Park)

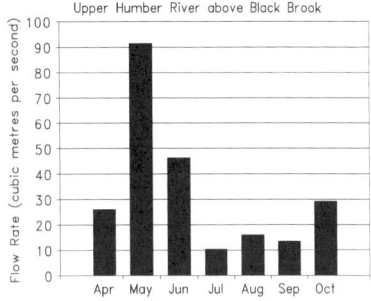

Upper Humber River above Black Brook

Flow Rate (cubic metres per second)

Apr May Jun Jul Aug Sep Oct

RAPIDS: Class 1-2 depending on water level.

WATER NOTES: This is a great route to do with your family. Strong southwesterly winds can make paddling difficult on some sections of the river.

DISTANCE: 50+ km (31+ mi.).

DURATION: 3-4 days.

DESCRIPTION: If you want to experience a canoe trip that captures the beauty of western Newfoundland, this is the one. With only 15 km (9 mi.) between the entry and egress, it is ideal for individuals who do not want the hassles of car shuttling. Although the trip can be completed with 2 days of hard paddling, plan to spend at least 3 or even 4 nights on the river. The Humber River is a licensed salmon river, so obtain a salmon licence if you plan to do any fishing.

At one time, the Humber and many of its tributaries were used to run logs to Deer Lake and on to the Bowater paper mill in Corner Brook. Much evidence, ranging from old booms, chains, dams and camps, can be found along the route. These reminders evoke images of the great days of the log drive.

The bridge across Dead Water Brook is the beginning of your trip and a place to watch spawning salmon and trout in late summer and early fall. From here, Dead Water Brook meanders through lowlands to Adies Lake. The brook is narrow in some places and in summer quite shallow, requiring the paddler to get out and wade. Trout are numerous, but do not take out your rod since Dead Water Brook is closed to fishing all year round. On the southeast shore of Adies Lake, there are beautiful sand beaches ideally suited for camping. Because of the east/west orientation of the lake, predominantly westerly winds can result in very high waves especially near the eastern end of the lake. Consider hugging the south shore as you make your way across in windy weather. It is often a wise decision to paddle an extra few kilometres for safety's sake.

Adies Stream begins at the east end of the lake. An old dam once used to control water levels when the Bowater Pulp and Paper company ran logs down the Humber marks the beginning of Adies Stream. Much of the dam has now fallen into ruin. A slick of fast water running between an old chute in the dam can be run. Keep to the left or right to avoid a large rock just below the surface. Adies Stream winds its way to the Humber. Along its banks old fishing lodges can be found, some of which are still in use. Reportedly, Queen Elizabeth spent some time in one of these lodges before she became queen. All the rapids on Adies Stream can be safely run. When you reach Cleary's Island, to avoid broaching on a series of rocks, take the right branch around the island and swing left with the river when you run the fast water.

Approximately 20 km (12 mi.) from Adies Lake, Adies Stream joins the Humber. If you have time, paddle up the Humber, portage over a dam and you will be in Birchy

Basin. Considerable work has been done in the basin by Ducks Unlimited to enhance the duck habitat. Birchy Basin is a bird watcher's heaven: ducks, Canada geese and many other species of birds abound.

At the junction of Adies Stream and the Humber (called "the Forks" by local residents), the river swings southwest. You will encounter a Class 1 rapid on river right as you enter the Humber. Approximately 200 metres (656 ft.) further downstream on river left is the confluence of Gales Brook and the Humber River. At low water the sandspit at the mouth of Gales Brook makes for an ideal campsite. Westerly winds may provide you with a challenging paddle on this section of the river. Follow your map carefully. Just past Alder Pond, the river opens into many channels—keep left to avoid getting lost. You will pass River Side, an old logging camp and site where logs were once dumped into the Humber to begin the long run to the mill in Corner Brook. It is approximately 23 km (14 mi.) from the forks to the first set of rapids, called Bear Reef. It is advised that you line the reef. A friend of ours who has done many trips down the Humber has yet to run the reef successfully. It seems that you are just about to clear it when your canoe will hang up. With the large volume of water going over the ledge this predicament can lead to serious consequences. You will pass 2 more sets of rapids which should be scouted before you reach Sir Richard Squires Park.

Approach Big Falls with extreme caution. The best way to get over them is to eddy out along the left side of the river and line your canoe until you reach the lip of the falls. The rocks are slippery and the current is fast. Here, there is a fish ladder that has been blasted into the rock. Carry your canoe over the large flat rocks and then you can either continue or carry your gear up a set of stairs and find a camp site.

LOGISTICS: Take Highway 1 west from Corner Brook to Deer Lake. Past Deer Lake, take Route 430, the Viking Trail, north. You will pass over the Humber River. Approximately 2 km (1.25 mi.) past the bridge, take Route 42 to Cormack. Travel 20 km (12 mi.) through Cormack and then take a left on a woods road. The road will take you to Dead Water Brook, the entry point for this trip. You may have some difficulty finding this road, so check with the local residents if unsure. Although this trip is over 50 km (31 mi.) in length, the entry and egress points are only 15 km (9 mi.) apart.

MAPS: 12H/6, 12H/11.

CHARTS: N/A.

Lunch stop on Adies Stream.

Humber River (Sir Richard Squires Memorial Park to Deer Lake)

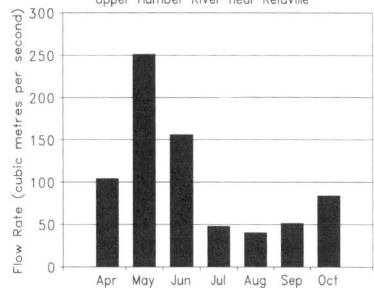

Upper Humber River near Reidville

RAPIDS: Class 1-2.

WATER NOTES: Like all rivers on the west coast, season and recent rainfall will determine the difficulty of this stretch of river. Generally, this section of the Humber can be paddled by a canoeist with intermediate white water skills.

DISTANCE: 30 km (19 mi.).

DURATION: 1 day (steady paddling) or 2 days ideal.

DESCRIPTION: This is one of the most enjoyable sections of the Humber River. The shallow meandering river winds through the upper section of the Humber Valley. Many well-known salmon pools are found along this section of the river, so it is not uncommon to pass salmon fishermen trying their luck during the open season.

Soon after leaving Sir Richard Squires Memorial Park, you will encounter Little Falls, located directly under a bridge. Little Falls can be run along the left, but should be scouted first or lined along the right. Approximately 5 km (3 mi.) past Little Falls, there is a series of shallow rapids. The first is Paddy's Reef followed by Crooked Reef 2.5 km (1.5 mi.) after, and another 1.5 km (1 mi.) paddle will bring you to Camp 9 Reef. Expect to get out and pull your canoe unless water levels are high. This set of rapids terminates at Harriman's Steady.

Below Harriman's Steady is Drillhole Rapids and then Cache Rapids, both of which are Class 2. Keep left when running the Cache Rapids during low water. From the Cache Rapids, it is a 2 km (1.25 mi.) paddle to the community of Reidsville and an additional 8 km (5 mi.) to Deer Lake.

If you run this section of the river during salmon season, expect to encounter up to 30 or more salmon fishermen at some of the more popular holes. Let them know that you are coming and attempt to stay clear. If you plan to paddle on to Deer Lake, consider staying at the community park, which can be accessed by paddling south along the lake. Be careful, since waves at this end of the lake may exceed 1 m (3.3 ft.) during windy weather. While they are excellent to play and surf in, they can provide a real challenge if you are trying to traverse them. If you plan to paddle the lake, it is about 19 km (12 mi.) to Boom Siding and will take you about 4 hours.

LOGISTICS: Access to Sir Richard Squires Memorial Park is gained by taking highway 430, the Viking Trail, 2 km (1.25 mi.) north to Route 42 through the farming area of Cormack. Approximately 30 km (19 mi.) down the road is Sir Richard Squires Park. Plan to spend a night in the park. During the salmon run, salmon can be seen jumping the falls. The ideal place to put-in is at the Little Falls Bridge that crosses the Humber approximately 4 km (2.5 mi.) before the park.

MAPS: 12H/6, 12H/3.

CHART: N/A.

Humber River (Deer Lake to the Humber Arm)

Humber River @ Humber Village Bridge (Regulated)

Flow Rate (cubic metres per second): Apr ~325, May ~450, Jun ~335, Jul ~190, Aug ~200, Sep ~195, Oct ~245

RAPIDS: Class 1.

WATER NOTES: Fairly easy paddling except when there is a challenging headwind.

DISTANCE: 19 km (12 mi.).

DURATION: 3-4 hours.

DESCRIPTION: The lower section of the Humber River winds through the scenic Humber Valley. On both sides heavily forested hills rise to 600 m (1900 ft.). In late September and October, these hills are ablaze with the reds and golds of fall, offering the perfect backdrop for a day's outing. As you glide down the river, you will pass many cabins and a few large strawberry farms which border the river's edge, a testament to the fertility of the Humber Valley soils. The community of Steady Brook lies on the left bank and, in the distance, you will see Marble Mountain, a popular ski resort. From this point, the Trans Canada Highway winds along the left bank of the river. Its lower portion offers an easy paddle until you reach Shellbird Island. Legend has it that years ago, pirates buried their treasure on this small island. At this point, you will encounter some rather interesting fast water. Depending on the tide and the level of the river, Shellbird Rapids will vary from a simple challenge to a serious one with 0.5 to 1 m (1.6 to 3.3 ft.) standing waves. I know of a few paddlers who tipped their canoe at these rapids and were washed right to the salt water before they were rescued. Expect an audience when you run these rapids, since they run right along side the Trans Canada Highway. Below the rapids, the Humber rushes through a small canyon with vertical rock walls rising on either side. The river undercuts the rock wall on the left side and, depending on the tide, there may a number of whirlpools, so beware. In addition, predominantly westerly wind funnelling up the Humber Valley can give your arms and shoulders a good workout.

LOGISTICS: Access to the lower portion of the Humber River is gained by travelling east along Highway 1 towards Deer Lake. Boom Siding is the ideal spot to launch if you do not want to do any paddling in Deer Lake. South Brook Park provides the best entry site. The park offers overnight camping and the opportunity to do some paddling on the lake. There is an approximate 5 km (3 mi.) paddle from South Brook Park to the mouth of the Humber.

MAP: 12A/13.

CHART: N/A.

Grand Lake - Sandy Lake - Birchy Lake

RAPIDS: N/A.

WATER NOTES: These are the largest inland bodies of water on the island. Because of their size and cold waters, they should be given the same respect as the ocean.

DISTANCE:
- O West end of Grand Lake to Birchy Lake - 150 km (95 mi.) (via Sandy Lake);
- O Northern Harbour, west end of Grand Lake, Deer Lake Loop - 125 km (77 mi.);
- O West end of Grand Lake to Humber Arm - 150 km (93 mi.) (via Deer Lake).*

    * Paddling the Humber River requires some river experience.

DURATION: 4-8 days.

DESCRIPTION: In 1925, Grand Lake was dammed to provide hydroelectric power for the paper mill in Corner Brook. Construction of a dam on Junction Brook resulted in the water level of Grand Lake being raised about 8.5 m (28 ft.), flooding many of the older beaches but also creating new ones. The diverted water passes through a powerhouse located in the community of Deer Lake. The tailrace runs into Deer Lake, into the Humber River and on to the Bay of Islands.

In some ways, Grand Lake is like the ocean, experiencing very high waves when the winds are westerly and its size and volume contribute to the coolness of the water even in mid-summer. Vertical cliffs bordering the lake rise to approximately 500 m (1600 ft.). These cliffs, which limit take-outs and campsites, provide spectacular backdrops for the many waterfalls cascading into the lake below, especially after a summer's rain.

On one clear, calm, moonlit night while camped at the mouth of a brook running into the west end of Grand Lake, we were awakened by the sound of hooves on the cobble beach at 1:00 in the morning. We peered out of our tent and, to our surprise, no more than 3 m (10 ft.) from our tent stood 2 moose. "What a spectacular sight," we thought, until we were reminded that "they're so blind they might walk right over us."

Through the Long Range Mountains, the wind blows and funnels, creating completely unpredictable wind conditions on the water. Sometimes, conditions change from dead calm to hurricane-like in minutes, as was the case on the night we were visited by the pair of moose. With the limited space, we had pitched the tent 3 m (10 ft.) from the shore. At 5:00 AM, waves created by the high winds were lapping precariously close to the tent door.

In the middle of Grand Lake is Glover Island, 20 km (24 mi.) long. It is the home of moose, majestic stands of balsam fir, black spruce and, according to some recent findings, gold. Interestingly, Glover Island contains another lake with an island. Surrounding the Grand Lake is one of the province's few last stands of old growth forest and one of the last remaining habitats of the pine marten.

Grand Lake to Deer Lake is connected by the Humber Canal which is approximately 14 km (9 mi.) long. About 5 km (3 mi.) into the canal, you will encounter the control structure. On the downstream end of this dam, the eddies can be very powerful as the flow increases. The water flow pattern will vary depending on the number of gates open. An additional 8 km paddle will bring you to Deer Lake. The portage through the community of Deer Lake is easiest by truck but can be managed on foot. The portage takes you close to Main Street, so park your canoe and go visit some of the local shops!

Paddling east on Grand Lake will bring you past Junction Brook. According to J.B. Juke, a Nineteenth century explorer, Micmacs making their way up from Bay St. George massacred a village of Beothucks somewhere at the north end of the lake. Paddling on through Main Brook between Grand Lake and Sandy Lake is a test of map and compass skills, since there are many islands and inlets, a great place to explore on a warm summer's day. As you paddle on through Sandy and Birchy Lakes, you will notice more evidence of civilization, shallower, warmer waters and plenty of sandy beaches. For those of you with a voyageur spirit, you can continue through Sandy Lake, Birchy Lake and, with a portage, catch the head waters of Indian River as it flows from Lake Buck, and continue on to Springdale and Halls Bay.

Grand Lake and beyond will appeal to those who are looking for an extended lake water trip with few or no portages—something difficult to find in this province.

LOGISTICS: Gallants: take the dirt road directly across from the turn-off to Gallants. Follow it to the end approximately 5 km (3 mi.) and you will arrive at the west end of Grand Lake. The road is narrow and partially grown in, so expect to have alders scraping along the side of your car or truck.

Northern Harbour: in Pasadena, turn off the Trans Canada Highway towards Holy Rosary School. Continue straight through the first intersection and you will be on the North Harbour road which takes you directly to the shore of Grand Lake.

Sandy and Birchy Lakes: both lakes can be accessed where they intersect with the Trans Canada Highway approximately 40 km (25 mi.) east of Deer Lake or from Highway 401 leading to Howley.

MAPS: 12B/9, 12A/12, 12A/13, 12A/14, 12H/3, 12H/2, 12H/7.

CHART: N/A.

Effects of flooding on Grand Lake.

Canyons, Coves and Coastal Waters

Mark Gerin

Jumping Pillow Falls on the Terra Nova River during the taping of the CBC Land and Sea episode "White Water Adventures."

Jim Price

A glimpse from inside a cave, Cape Broyle.

Kevin Redmond

Coastal waters of Bonavista Bay.

Kevin Redmond

Big Steady, Main River.

Mark Dykeman

Riding "The Haystacks," Main River.

Linda Bartlett

Indian River family tripping.

Kevin Redmond

Sea kayaking on the West Coast.

Kevin Redmond

Hiking the long range near headwaters of Main River.

Western Brook fjord from 5000 feet.

Stag Brook, Gros Morne.

St. Paul's Inlet.

Tippens Pond (Massey Drive Pond)

RAPIDS: N/A.

WATER NOTES: Flat water.

DISTANCE: Tippens Pond is approximately 0.5 km (0.3 mi.) long and 0.25 km (0.1 mi.) wide.

DURATION: Day trip or short paddle.

DESCRIPTION: On your way to the Main River? Passing through and spending a night in Corner Brook? If so, plan a drive to Tippens Pond, or Massey Drive Pond as it is called by the locals. This little pond offers you a great opportunity for a leisurely paddle and the possibility of meeting some local paddlers.

Tippens Pond is the site of the Long Range Canoe Club's facilities. There are 3 wharves located along the shores of the pond, a T-shaped wharf on the west side from which you can launch your canoe and 2 more docks on the south side of the lake. The latter are used for teaching platforms when canoe courses are being taught, but they also provide the perfect place to fish from or to just lie in the sun on a hot summer's day. Do not forget to bring your fly rod. Pan-sized speckled trout are found in the lake and when they are biting, you may be rewarded with a fresh meal. The lake is located about 260 m (800 ft.) above sea level, so bring an extra sweater, even in mid-summer, since the temperature is cool.

LOGISTICS: Access to Tippens Pond is via the Massey Drive overpass off the Trans Canada Highway. Take the turn to the community of Massey Drive and drive approximately 2 km (1.5 mi.) through the community. You cannot miss the pond because it is located at the very end of the road across from the Rod and Gun Club. A long T-shaped wharf is located at this end of the pond where you can launch your canoe or kayak.

MAP: 12A/13.

CHART: N/A.

Canoe instruction, Tippens Pond.

Wild Cove

RAPIDS: N/A, ocean paddling.

WATER NOTES: Wild Cove is located at the upper end of the Humber arm. Like all saltwater paddling routes on the west coast the cove is susceptible to westerly and southwesterly winds. Morning and evening paddlers are usually rewarded with mirror-like waters and beautiful sunsets. If you plan to paddle during midday, beware that the wind can come up within minutes, so check the weather before you depart.

DISTANCE: 2 km (1.2 mi.).

DURATION: Day trip or short paddle

DESCRIPTION: Wild Cove is the ideal site for a short paddle or a one day excursion. Paddling left from the launch site at Prince Edward Park will take you past a series of rocky beaches at the bottom of a high bluff. At low tide, you will see a sand bar on your right as you round the bend. According to local historians, a pirate ship was driven aground here while being pursued by a British warship. The crew abandoned ship and made their way up the Humber River, burying their precious treasure on Shellbird Island. The current will increase as you paddle your way towards the mouth of the Humber River.

Paddling from the launch will take you across a shallow bay and along a rocky shore. Here, the remains of an old barge can be found, reminders of the early days of floating pulp wood to the mill via river and sea. Continuing along the shore, the waters become very shallow as you approach the mouth of Huges Brook. When the tide is high you can paddle up Huges Brook and see a variety of ducks and other bird life. Further upstream, a local salmon enhancement project has been ongoing for a number of years and is well worth a look. If the weather and winds are favourable, paddle further up the shore past the communities of Irish Town and Summerside.

In the evenings, you will experience stunning sunsets over the Bay of Islands. Consider a night paddle on a warm summer's night: an excellent way to top off a day on the water. The lights of Corner Brook and the surrounding communities shimmer and glisten on the bay's surface.

LOGISTICS: Access to Wild Cove is gained by travelling highway 440. You will pass over the Humber River. Approximately 1 km (0.6 mi.) past the bridge, you will see the entrance to Prince Edward Park on your left. The park offers reasonable over-night camping rates. Access to the water is via a boat launch located at the west end of the park. There is a small fee for launching canoes and sea kayaks. If you do not want to launch from the park, travelling an additional kilometre will bring you close to the water's edge. Across from the Department of Highway's depot, you will see an old, grown-over trail leading down to the salt water. When the tide is out, there is a mud flat, so you will have to carry your canoe or kayak to the water's edge.

Highway 440 runs up along most of the north shore of the bay allowing easy access for those interested in paddling sections of the bay.

MAP: 12A/13.

CHART: 4653.

Wood's Island

RAPIDS: N/A, ocean paddling.

WATER NOTES: Winds and waves will be your biggest concern when sea kayaking or canoeing this area. When the winds come up, the larger 6 m open fishing boats often become windbound on Wood's Island. Waves refracting around the island from the west result in unpredictable wave patterns on the east side of the island.

DISTANCE: ○ 2 km (1.2 mi.) offshore via McIver's Point;

○ 3 km (1.9 mi.) offshore via Shoal Point.

DURATION: Day trip or weekend excursion.

DESCRIPTION: Wood's Island was the site of one of the first settlements in the Bay of Islands and was resettled in the early 1960s. Today, many of the families still return to the Island, staying in their cabins tucked around the harbour and throughout the island. Old walking trails abound, leading you to grave yards, foundations and grassy fields, reminders of bygone days. The island provides a perfect destination for a day or weekend of exploration. It is hard to describe this picture in words. Wood's Island harbour is surrounded by lush green fields and guarded by two natural breakwaters. To the south, the Blow-Me-Down Mountains reach skyward. All of this can be found just a few kilometres from Corner Brook.

Along the northwest end of the island lies a series of 7 smaller, rocky outcrops called the Puffin Islands. During certain times of the year, minke whales and seals visit these waters to play and feed.

LOGISTICS: To access from the north shore, travel highway 440 to the community of McIver's. Launch your kayak and paddle up the shore to McIver's Point. From here, it is less than a 2 km (1.2 mi.) paddle to the island. The waters here are cold in any season, so it is best to don your wet or dry suit and paddle with a partner. This route lies east of the island and offers shelter from westerly winds. However, you many experience strange wave patterns as the waves refract around the island from the west. Paddle up the south side of the island to Wood Island's harbour and enjoy.

For access from the south shore, travel highway 450 to Frenchman's Cove and launch your kayak here. Paddle up the left shore to Shoal Point and across to the island.

MAP: 12G/1.

CHART: 4653.

York Harbour - Lark Harbour - Bottle Cove

RAPIDS: N/A, ocean paddling.

WATER NOTES: Beware of those westerly and southwesterly winds and cold waters, especially if you are a novice paddler.

DISTANCE: 2-10 km (1.2-6 mi.) depending on route.

DURATION: Day trips.

DESCRIPTION: This area of the Bay of Islands will provide you with a series of short, but delightful day paddles. Making your base at Blow-Me-Down Provincial Park puts you within minutes of many exciting paddling and hiking routes. Both York Harbour and Lark Harbour, named after Captain James Cook's ships the Lark and York, are sheltered from the south-westerly and westerly winds.

Two small islands, Governors Island and Seal Island, are found within York Harbour. These islands were used by the Basque whalers as bases during their summer visits to the west coast in search of fish, whales and seals. Seal Island lies just below Blow-Me-Down Mountain which rises almost 610 m (2000 ft.) straight up. Strong southerly winds coming over the mountain often result in an incredible down draft, turning the waters around Seal Island into a wild spray.

When the weather is fine, you will be able to paddle most of the coast in these areas. In the west, Murray Mountains reach skyward and, in the distance, Guernsey Island seems to almost hover near the entrance to the Bay of Islands.

Bottle Cove, on the other hand, is exposed to the southwest, so pick a calm day or evening before venturing out of the cove. Explore the huge sea cave (on your left as you leave the harbour), the rock formations and the majestic cliffs along this rugged but beautiful coast line.

LOGISTICS: Bottle Cove, York Harbour and Lark Harbour can be easily reached by taking Route 450 out of Corner Brook. Before leaving the city, stop at Cook's Monument located high on top of Crow Hill. Captain James Cook was responsible for charting much of the west coast including the Bay of Islands. A brass copy of his chart is mounted on a stone monument here. Travelling west, you will pass through many small communities and then along the base of the Blow-Me-Down Mountains.

MAP: 12G/1.

CHART: 4654.

Indian River

RAPIDS: Class 1.

WATER NOTES: The Indian River is truly a recreational river ideally suited to the novice paddler. With its shallow to deep water and moderate current, the river is subject to variable seasonal water levels. Expect to drag your canoe in some places if the river is paddled in mid summer. Even in late May, the water can be very shallow along some sections of the river.

DISTANCE: ○ Bridge on the Baie Verte Highway 41 to Springdale - 42 km (20 mi);
○ Indian River Provincial Park to Springdale - 25 km (15 mi.).

DURATION: 1-2 days.

DESCRIPTION: Indian River offers an ideal paddling route for the beginner canoeist or the expert who would like to take family and friends on a relatively easy paddle. The river gets its name from the fact that Maritime Archaic Indians once lived and fished at Indian River Falls near Springdale.

If you are planning to spend 2 nights on the river, consider spending a night at Indian River Provincial Park. Access to the park from the river involves a rather strenuous climb to the top of the bluff where the park is located. For those who prefer the tranquil solitude of the Newfoundland wilderness, there are many suitable campsites along the river.

There are 2 portages on the river. The first is around a salmon enhancement project just a short distance after you enter the river from the old Baie Verte Provincial Park. If you have time, stop and have a chat with the people working on the enhancement project. I am sure they will give you some background on the project and insight into the amazing life cycle of the Atlantic salmon. The second portage is at Indian Falls just before you reach Springdale. You should approach the falls with caution along the left bank. Missing the exit point will result in serious consequences. You may want to continue your paddle to the ocean (Hall's Bay) or camp at the community park at the falls. The middle section of the river parallels the Trans Canada Highway so, if a problem arises, help is not too far off.

LOGISTICS: There are a number of access points. The old Baie Verte Provincial Park, 2 km (1.2 mi.) west of the Baie Verte turnoff, is an ideal access point, providing the longest trip. The park provides a picturesque camp site for your first night. Other access points include the bridge on the Baie Verte Highway (Route 410) and Indian River Provincial Park for a shorter paddle.

MAPS: 12H/8 , 12H 7.

CHART: N/A.

Quiet day on Indian River.

Pinchgut Lake to Georges Lake

RAPIDS: Class 1-2 (depending on season).

WATER NOTES: Approximately 2 km (1.2 mi.) down stream is a private bridge. During high water, it is impossible for a canoe to squeeze underneath, so be prepared to exit above the bridge and carry over.

DISTANCE: 4 km (2.5 mi.).

DURATION: 45 minutes.

DESCRIPTION: This is a popular first white water run of the season for many canoeists in the Corner Brook area. In early and mid-May, the river swells with icy cold water as meltwater from the winter snows rush down from the highlands. A short paddle down the river will take you to a bridge on the Trans Canada Highway where you may exit or continue down to Pinchgut Lake. Continuing on the lake requires an additional 2 km (1.2 mi.) paddle through consistent Class 1-1.5 rapids, depending on the season. You enter Georges Lake at Camp Stanfield. The water is very shallow and south-westerly winds coming down the lake can be tricky. Paddle left to the highway where you can make your egress.

LOGISTICS: Travel the Trans Canada Highway west past Pinchgut Lake approximately 15 km (9 mi.) west of Corner Brook. As you pass the south end of the lake, look for a woods road on your left. Travel down this road until you reach a bridge crossing Pinchgut Stream and enter the river there.

MAPS: 12B/16, 12A/13.

CHART: N/A.

Early Bird Run on Harrys River.

Canyons, Coves and Coastal Waters

Harrys River

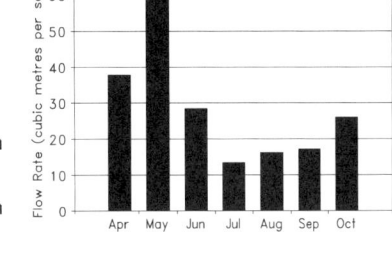

Harry's River below Highway Bridge

RAPIDS: Class 1 and 2 rapids, depending on water level.

WATER NOTES: This can be a wild river in early spring so paddle with caution.

DISTANCE:
- ○ Georges Lake to Gallants - approx. 5 km (3 mi.);
- ○ Gallants to Black Duck - approx. 17 km (10 mi.);
- ○ Black Duck to Georges Bay - approx. 10 km (6 mi.).

DURATION:
- ○ Georges Lake to Gallants - 1-2 hours;
- ○ Gallants to Black Duck - 3-4 hours;
- ○ Black Duck to Georges Bay - 2 hours.

DESCRIPTION: Picture this: a large company of canoeists gathered at Gallants bridge, dressed in the best of gear, gortex fluttering in the wind and a mirage of colours—reds, safety orange and yellows. Locals began to gather to witness this strange event. What must they have thought as the first canoe pulled out of an eddy, through the first standing wave and swamped in front of them! As we were being flushed downstream, we looked back to see them running along the river's edge, hoping to save us. They never did catch us. The swift waters carried us down to the junction of North Brook and Harrys. Our paddling partners retrieved our canoe 1 km (0.6 mi.) down stream.

Harrys is a beautiful paddling river. Running approximately 37 km (23 mi.) from Georges Lake to the ocean, it offers both the novice and experienced paddler a challenging run. In the spring, there is consistent fast water from beginning to end. Trees along the river banks are scarred up to 2 m (6 ft.) above the normal water level, a testimony to the power of the ice moving down river during spring breakup. You are sure to see moose and other forms of wildlife as you paddle along this beautiful river.

LOGISTICS: You have a number of choices of where to begin this trip. If the winds are light and you have time for a lake paddle, consider putting in at the north end of Georges Lake, approximately 30 km (19 mi.) south of Corner Brook along the Trans Canada Highway. It is approximately a 10 km (6 mi.) paddle down the lake to where Harrys begins.

If you would like to pass on the lake paddle, then continue another 10 km (6 mi.) along the Trans Canada Highway and turn right to Gallants. About 5 km (3 mi.) down this road, you come to the small community of Gallants and pass over a bridge on the Harrys River. Put-in here or continue right on a dirt road to the south end of Georges Lake where the Harrys river begins. If you plan to take-out at Black Duck Siding, there is a 50 km (31 mi.) round trip car shuttle between Black Duck Siding and the Gallants Bridge.

Located in the same area is Blue Ponds Park, a great place to spend a night.

MAPS: 12B/16, 12B/9.

CHART: N/A.

Gros Morne National Park
(East and South Arm)

RAPIDS: N/A, ocean and lake paddling.

WATER NOTES: Open water prone to westerly and south-westerly winds.

DURATION: Day trips or multiday trips.

DESCRIPTION: Western Newfoundland is blessed with Gros Morne National Park. Established in 1973 and declared a UNESCO World Heritage Site in 1987, the park is a portal into the earth's crust. This geological wonderland has been thrust up from the earth below, scoured by glaciers, washed by rains, heated by the summer's sun and dusted with winter's frost for thousands of years. The result is a hiker's and paddler's wonderland.

Both the South and East Arms, partially located within the boundaries of Gros Morne National Park, offer a selection of fine paddling routes for the visiting sea kayaker or coastal canoeist. Although both arms are relatively narrow and protected from the Gulf of St. Lawrence, strong westerlies can make paddling rather challenging, so check the weather before your trip. If the winds do pick up, try to stay near the sheltered shores of the arms, since the high hills provide a wind shadow effect. If you plan to spend more than a day exploring the arms, remember that parts of them lie within the boundaries of the park and you are allowed to camp only in designated areas. Before beginning your trip, check in with the park office. No permit is required, but it is wise to let them know your route.

Lomond, located at the head of East Arm, will easily satisfy the most ardent paddler. Lomond was once a thriving community. Logs running down the Lomond River were boomed here and towed to the Bowater Mill in Corner Brook or shipped directly overseas. Time and resettlement have erased all but a few relics of this once prosperous community. A short paddle to the west of Lomond, nestled in a valley between 2 hills, is the community of Stanleyville. Rusting hulks of metal and the outlines of old root cellars are all that remain of this community.

Begin your paddling trip from the public wharf at Lomond and then paddle the 4 km (2.5 mi.) up the shore to your right towards the mouth of the Lomond River. The waters here are shallow, particularly at low tide. Your reward will be a menagerie of birds that inhabit the region of the arm. Lomond River is also a licensed salmon river, so do not be surprised if you see a fisherman trying his luck. Leave the mouth of the Lomond and continue across the end of the arm. On our last trip, the waters were as smooth as a plate of glass. Gazing down, we could see sea urchins, crabs, starfish and many other forms of marine life that inhabit these cool northern waters. Within the first 2 km (1.2 mi.), we saw 3 mature bald eagles who we suspect were nesting on the cliffs above and keeping a close eye on this strange cigar shaped craft. A short paddle will take you to the mouth of South East Brook. If the tide is out, you will be able to cross directly, in very shallow waters, over to the entry point and then up the shore to Stanleyville for lunch. Continuing up the shore will take you to Norris Point and Neddy Harbour. You must make arrangements to get back to Lomond if this is the termination of your day trip.

South Arm also offers some interesting paddling. Along the south side of the arm are the communities of Glenburnie, Birchy Head, Shoal Brook and Woody Point, which lie outside the park boundaries. The north shore of the arm lies within the park.

No trip to Gros Morne Park is complete without a trip down Western Brook Pond. With cliffs rising to over 650 m (2100 ft.) and waters plunging to a depth of 165 m (540 ft.), its beauty and grandeur will leave you breathless. A tour boat operates on the pond offering daily excursions for a nominal fee. If you are considering paddling Western Brook Pond a word of warning: the park does not encourage paddling Western Brook Pond, and the trip is limited to the experienced paddler. Strong winds, limited landing points and even falling rock can be disastrous. Although the tour boat runs twice daily, it usually will cancel trips if the weather is bad. It is possible to be windbound at the end of the pond or, worse still, on a narrow rocky shore with no room to pitch a tent or no way to walk out. One option is to have the tour boat transport your kayak down to the end of the pond and then, making your base camp at the wilderness site, spend a day or two hiking and paddling. When you find that you cannot take any more of this beauty and grandeur, come back on the tour boat or paddle back if winds are favourable.

LOGISTICS: Access to East Arm is from anywhere along Route 430, as it passes right along the north edge of East Arm or from the community of Norris Point. Taking Route 431 at Wiltondale will bring you to Lomond, just 13 km (8mi.) down the highway. Continuing further along Route 431 will bring you to Glenburnie at the head of South Arm.

Western Brook Pond is reached by continuing up Route 430 past the turn off to Rocky Harbour. You cannot miss the parking area located at the trail head. The pond is reached via a 2 km (1.2 mi.) walking trail. If you are going to bring your kayak in to the pond, consider rigging up some kind of trolley to wheel it in.

MAPS: 12H/5, 12H/12.

CHART: 4658.

A view of Gros Morne Mountain from Lomond.

Trout River Pond

RAPIDS: N/A.

WATER NOTES: Flat water exposed to westerly winds.

DISTANCE: 30 km (17 mi.) (round trip).

DURATION: 1 day or overnight.

DESCRIPTION: Trout River Pond is located within the boundaries of Gros Morne National Park and within 1 km (0.6 mi.) of the picturesque community of Trout River. Since the pond lies within park boundaries, the necessary camping permits must be acquired from the park's office in Rocky Harbour before you begin your trip. Trout River Pond is approximately 15 km (9 mi.) long with tablelands rising 610 m (2,000 ft.) on either side, especially towards the eastern end of the lake. These cliffs do not come to the edge of the pond as they do at Western Brook Pond; thus, there are many places to land if the winds come up. The route is well suited for sea kayak or open canoe. An ideal campsite is situated on the left of a narrowing between outer and inner Trout River Pond, 5 km (3 mi.) from the put-in. At the far end of the lake is a sandy beach, the perfect spot to relax after a long day's paddle. There is also a fully serviced campground at the west end of the lake. Do not forget to bring your hiking boots and day pack since there are many routes to the top of the surrounding tablelands.

LOGISTICS: Take Route 431 at Wiltondale and travel approximately 50 km (30 mi.) to the community of Trout River. Turn left, and continue until you reach a boat launch and recreation area administered by Parks Canada.

MAPS: 12G/8, 12G/5.

CHART: N/A.

Kevin Redmond

A child's first solo paddle, Trout River Pond.

North Arm - Penguin Arm - Goose Arm

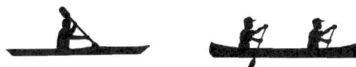

RAPIDS: N/A, ocean paddling.

WATER NOTES: Although these arms are relatively narrow, their east/west orientations make them susceptible to westerly winds.

DISTANCE: Varies depending on route selection.

DURATION: 1-2 days.

DESCRIPTION: These three arms are extensions of the beautiful Bay of Islands. At one time, the whole area was logged and the logs were boomed and towed to the paper mill in Corner Brook. An old wharf and rock-filled cribs for attaching booms can still be seen at the head of Goose Arm. The scenery here is spectacular. To the north, you will see mountains rising to 747 m (2,450 ft.) with no vegetation growing on them.

Goose Arm is approximately 12 km (7.5 mi.) long and Penguin Arm about 8 km (5 mi.). The ideal paddling route is to put-in at the head of Goose Arm and then paddle out and around into Penguin Arm for a total round trip of about 40 km (25 mi.). Camping sites are found at the head of Goose Arm and Penguin Arm.

LOGISTICS: There are 2 access points to this area. Travel on Route 440 from Corner Brook to the community of Cox's Cove. Cox's Cove lies on Middle Arm, with Goose Arm and Penguin Arm branching off from there. North Arm can be accessed by paddling around the headlands of Middle Arm. Paddling in rather exposed ocean waters is necessary especially to reach North Arm. On one occasion, a group of sea kayakers were windbound in Goose Arm for a number of days, so be aware of the weather. Since the return trip requires that you paddle west, problems may arise as westerly winds pick up during the day.

Penguin Arm and Goose Arm can also be accessed from their eastern ends via a well maintained woods road. Take Route 430 from Corner Brook and turn off into the community of Hughes Brook. Drive through the community until you reach a farm on your right. The pavement ends at the farm but continue on, keeping left until you get to Old Man's Pond. Here you will encounter a fork in the road. Take the right branch, continue straight for approximately 20 km (12 mi.) and soon you will arrive at the eastern end of Goose Arm. There is plenty of traffic on this old woods road so do not hesitate to stop somebody to ask for directions. The scenery along the route is spectacular.

MAPS: 12G/1, 12H/4.

CHART: 4653.

Stark, rugged beauty.

Sue Rendall

Serpentine River

RAPIDS: Class 1-2 depending on water level.

WATER NOTES: Located approximately 10 km (6 mi.) down river is a small falls which will require a portage. The lower section of the river may be very shallow in mid-summer.

DISTANCE: 20 km (12 mi.) from the west end of Serpentine Lake to the ocean.

DURATION: 2-3 days.

DESCRIPTION: Nestled between the Blow-Me-Down Mountains on the north and the Lewis Hills on the south lies Serpentine Lake and the Serpentine River. Serpentine lake is approximately 10 km (6 mi.) long and bordered by hills rising to 610 m (2,000 ft.) on the north and 330 m (1100 ft.) on the south. Some hikers and back country skiers say that the beauty of this area matches, if not surpasses, the beauty of Gros Morne National Park. The whole area is now under consideraton as Newfoundland and Labrador's third wilderness area.

The Serpentine River winds its way 20 km (12 mi.) to the ocean. The scenery along the river is magnificant. As you paddle closer to its mouth, the land begins to flatten and the current slows.

To your left in the distance, you will see spectacular Rope Cove Canyon cutting its way into the Lewis Hills. Just beyond the canyon is the highest spot on the island of Newfoundland, 814 m (2,670 ft.) above sea level. The Serpentine River is a scheduled salmon river. Make sure you obtain a salmon licence if you intend to do any fishing. Just above the falls, Bowater (the former owner of the pulp and paper mill in Corner Brook) used to maintain a fishing lodge. The lodge is now gone with only a few remains to be found.

LOGISTICS: Where the river enters the gulf, there is no access by road so you will have to arrange to be picked up by boat from Lark Harbour or Little Port. It is about a 15 km (9.3 mi.) run from the mouth of the Serpentine River to Little Port. The coast is exposed directly to the gulf and high cliffs limit landing areas. You should not paddle back along the coast unless you are sure that the waters and wind will remain calm for the trip.

To gain access to Serpentine Lake, travel approximately 20 km (12 mi.) south from Corner Brook on the Trans Canada Highway. Turn right onto an old woods road called Loggers School Road. Travel approximately 30 km (19 mi.) to the west end of Serpentine Lake. Here, you will find a Department of Fisheries cabin used by the river monitor during the salmon season. A 4-wheel drive or truck is needed since you will be required to drive around an old washed out bridge to reach the end of the lake.

MAP: 12B/16.

CHART: N/A.

Lloyds River

Lloyds River below King George IV Lake

(bar chart showing Flow Rate (cubic metres per second) from Apr to Oct: Apr ≈ 41, May ≈ 58, Jun ≈ 20, Jul ≈ 8, Aug ≈ 12, Sep ≈ 10, Oct ≈ 18)

RAPIDS: Classes 1-5 (the most difficult rapids are between King George IV Lake or Route 480 to Lloyds Lake).

WATER NOTES: With a very small water shed, this river is best paddled in spring or early summer. No matter where the paddler begins (King George IV lake, Burgeo highway or Lloyds Lake), the rapids generally get easier as the river runs east. Some dragging may be required in low-water areas.

DISTANCE: ○ King George IV Lake to Millertown - 140 km (87 mi.);

○ Route 480 to Millertown - 120 km (75 mi.).

DURATION: 3-6 days.

DESCRIPTION: When combined with the Exploits River, the Lloyds-Exploits River system is the largest in Newfoundland. Beginning within 50 km (31 mi.) of the Gulf of St. Lawrence, it traverses the island spilling into the Atlantic Ocean on the eastern edge. The headwaters of the Lloyds River are in an area of low relief with barren grounds dotted by small lakes and streams. For most of its length, the river flows parallel to the Annieopsquotch Mountains which rise steeply (up to 400 m (1300 ft.)) above the river valley.

The last obstacle before entering Lloyds Lake is a 6 km (4 mi.) series of rapids in the shadow of towering mountains on the right shore. This is followed by swift, shallow water and a wide selection of excellent campsites. The combination of eastern pine, birch, grassy meadows and river deltas before entering Lloyds Lake all helps create prime moose habitat and nesting grounds for ducks and Canada geese. In areas of narrow deep river channels, landlocked salmon called *ouananiche* and brook trout are plentiful.

From Lloyds Lake to Red Indian Lake, most rapids are minor in nature. More evidence of habitation indicates you are coming to Red Indian Lake, the second largest lake on the island.

Red Indian Lake is named after the Beothuck Indians that once lived in the area. The last Beothuck died in 1829, but many confirmed sites along Red Indian Lake and the Exploits are being excavated for Indian artifacts. When paddling on the lake, caution is recommended because of the lake's large size and cold water temperatures.

LOGISTICS: Take Route 480 off the Trans Canada Highway south of Stephenville. Drive to the bridge where the Lloyds River crosses the road. If you wish to put-in at either King George IV Lake or Lloyds Lake, follow the woods roads marked on the topographical maps west of the river. There are several egress points easily identifiable on these maps and they include the beginning of Red Indian Lake, Millertown Dam or Grand Falls if you wish to complete the whole system.

MAPS: N.T.S. Map Scale 1:250,000 12 A; N.T.S. Map Scale 1:50,000 12A/4, 12A/5, 12A/6, 12A/11, 12A/10, 12A/15.

CHART: N/A.

Barachois Brook

RAPIDS: Class 1 and 2 depending on the water level.

WATER NOTES: Barachois Brook, above Barachois Pond, is best run in early and late spring. The route from Barachois Pond to the ocean can be run throughout the summer, but expect to encounter areas through which you will need to drag.

DISTANCE: Barachois Brook to St. George's Bay - approximately 12 km (7.5 mi.).

DURATION: Day paddle.

DESCRIPTION: Barachois Brook is representative of the many rivers running out of this section of the Long Range Mountains. It is fast flowing in the spring, with water levels becoming almost uncanoeable in mid-summer. What makes the Barachois an ideal river is that it runs into Barachois Pond which is located within the boundaries of Barachois Provincial Park. Making your camp at the park, which is nestled at the base of the Long Range Mountains, you can easily drive along an old woods road to the upper reaches of the brook, put in almost anywhere and then run down to Barachois Pond. If you are heading up the west coast, especially in late spring or early summer, consider checking out the park and brook. It may be just what you are looking for after the trip across the gulf—a place to rest for a day and to get that road dust off your paddle and canoe.

LOGISTICS: Barachois Provincial Park is located right along the Trans Canada Highway, approximately 200 km (124 mi.) from Port-aux-Basques. Enter the park and travel approximatly 15 km (9 mi.) along the dirt road that parallels the river on the left. You can put your canoe in almost anywhere and enjoy.

MAPS: 12B/7, 12B/8.

CHART: N/A.

Lunchtime on Barachois Brook.

Grand Codroy River

RAPIDS: Classes 1 and 2 depending on water level.

WATER NOTES: Caution is advised (especially in high winds) on the open water at the mouth of the river.

DISTANCE: ○ South Branch to ocean - 28 km (17 mi.);

○ Coal Brook to ocean - 28 km (17 mi.);

○ North Branch to ocean - 48 km (30 mi.).

DURATION: 1-2 days.

DESCRIPTION: In contrast to the barren tundra, stunted forest and rockscape so prevalent throughout Newfoundland and Labrador, the Grand Codroy River Valley is lush and fertile. The valley was originally settled by the Micmac Indians who maintained themselves with agriculture and fishing. The Indians later shared the riches of the valley with white settlers before most of the Micmacs died from tuberculosis.

Beginning the trip near the community of South Branch at the base of the Long Range Mountains is appropiate as the river valley meanders through open pastures, grazing cattle, old farm buildings and a number of small rural settlements. Extensive white sand beaches coupled with the ocean and a warm, westerly saltwater breeze make a fitting conclusion to the trip.

At optimal water levels, the Grand Codroy below the confluence of the north and south branches can be an exciting run for the entry level river paddler. Within a half hour's drive from the Port aux Basques ferry terminal, the Grand Codroy is a scheduled salmon river with some breathtaking scenery. Adventurous paddlers have the option of running either the north or south branch of the river if adequate water is running. The diverse scenery of mountains, forest, pasture and seashore make this trip a pleasure for any paddler.

LOGISTICS: At high water levels, both the north and south branches of the river can be accessed where they cross the Trans Canada Highway. The south branch crosses the highway near the community of Coal Brook (approximately 55 km (34 mi.) north of Port aux Basques) and the north branch can be accessed just south of the community of North Branch (approximately 10 km (6 mi.) north of Coal Brook).

To access the crossing of the north and south branches, a 1 km (0.6 mi.) road through the community of South Branch will lead to the river's edge.

The take-out for the trip can be any of the small communities at the mouth of the river along the Gulf of St. Lawrence. The most identifiable feature is the bridge spanning the river between the communities of Upper Ferry and Great Codroy.

MAPS: N.T.S. Map Scale 1:50,000 11-0/14 includes confluence to ocean; 11-0/15 includes North and South Branches.

CHART: N/A.

Main River

Main River @ Paradise Pool

Flow Rate (cubic metres per second)

120 100 80 60 40 20 0

Apr May Jun Jul Aug Sep Oct

RAPIDS: Most rapids are from Class 1-3, but with heavy rains these can very quickly be transformed into Classes 4 and 5.

WATER NOTES: At low water, the 5 km (3 mi.) section above Big Steady can be frustrating and unpleasant, as the canoes have to be walked down a slippery boulder garden. Shin pads would be a definite asset.

DISTANCE: ○ Four Ponds to Sop's Arm - 57 km (35 mi.);

○ Woods road bridge to Sop's Arm - 23 km (14 mi.).

DURATION: ○ Four Ponds to Sop's Arm - 5-6 days;

○ Woods road bridge to Sop's Arm - 1-2 days.

DESCRIPTION: Scouting a rapid from high above the water level can be a recipe for disaster. As it turns out, we learned our lesson on our second trip on the Main. From high above the water, the plan was simple; sneak down the left to avoid the large standing waves in mid stream, slip to river right to miss the hole at the bottom of the ledge and we are in the clear. Even if we did not miss the hole, it did not look that big anyway. So much for depth perception!

We put our plan into action, but everything was different at water level. The canoe seemed heavier, the waves were higher and the hole was bigger—much bigger. As a result, we did not make the move to river right. We crashed through the hole and swamped. One of us managed to swim to the eddy immediately but because of the mistake, the other was sentenced to swimming the remaining 100 m (328 ft.) of rapids, thus ending up with two saucer sized bruises on the most padded part of his anatomy. The canoe wasn't so lucky. Full of gear and water, it dug in stern first under a large rock, stood on end and pitch poled down river tearing a 30 cm (12 in.) gash in its side.

Fortunately, the canoeist's #1 repair kit saved the day and, with a liberal application of duct tape to the Old Town and our pride, we continued on one of the most enjoyable canoe trips we can remember.

Although not a long river, the Main contains such a diversity of wilderness and canoeing experience that it is comparable, in many ways, to longer wild rivers in other parts of the world. The Main became the first Newfoundland river to be nominated as a Canadian Heritage River. Flowing clean and unobstructed from its headwaters in the heart of the Long Range Mountains, the Main courses southeast from tundra-like barrens, through expanses of softwood forests and a unique area of grass land called Big Steady, a critical habitat for a variety of wildlife and vegetation. The river completes its journey to the Atlantic through a spectacular 23 km (14 mi.) canyon.

The Main's "variety pack" of canoeing begins at Four Ponds Lake, the farthest point up river accessible only by float plane. These pleasant lakes are linked with short stretches of swift but relaxing water and give the opportunity to fish for Speckled trout or Atlantic salmon. Four Ponds to Big Steady is a mixture of small ledges and rock-studded boulder gardens. At low water, this stretch can be a frustrating drag, but at high water, it is an extremely delightful run through mostly Class 2 rapids. After a leisurely float through Big Steady, you encounter the area known as the rapid section.

Canyons, Coves and Coastal Waters

Granite reflections: Dog Island, Labrador.

Port Manvers Run in the rain.

Kevin Redmond

South Coast of Labrador.

Jim Price

A majestic sight.

Moisie River, Labrador and Quebec.

Exploring Igloo Island: Port Manvers Run, Labrador.

Geological wonders of Trout River Pond.

Maneuvering on the Main River.

Mostly pool and drop, it is considered one of the more challenging sections and boasts of Class 3, 4 and the odd Class 5 drop at high water. The canyon section, beginning where Big Brook enters the Main, is a continuous Class 2-3 roller coaster ride down a steep uniform gradient. This gradient of 10m/km (53 ft./mi.) is steeper than the usual limit of an open canoe. However, because of the consistency of drop, small size of the river and channel characteristics, most rapids are runnable with only occasional lining and portaging.

LOGISTICS: Access to one of the upper lakes is by float plane only. A woods road leading up river from Sop's Arm crosses the river approximately 2 km (1.2 mi.) into the canyon section.

Take-out is at Sop's Arm where the river meets the main highway near Sop's Arm Provincial Park.

MAPS: 12H/14, 12H/15.

CHART: N/A.

Sailing down Four Ponds.

Riding the haystacks in the canyon.

LABRADOR

Glacial Valley, Torngnat Mountains.

To the west was a series of lake expansions connected by narrow straits, and beyond them were the mountains which we estimated rose about 2500 ft above the country at their base. In sheltered places on their sides, patches of snow glistened in the sunshine. Barren almost to their base, not a vestige of vegetation to be seen anywhere on their tops or sides, they presented a scene of desolate grandeur, standing out against the blue sky like a grim barrier placed there to guard the land beyond. As I gazed upon them, some lines from Kipling's 'Explorer' that I had often heard Hubbard repeat were brought forcibly to my mind.

"Some thing hidden. Go find it. Go and look behind the Ranges. Something lost behind the Ranges. Lost and waiting for you. Go!'

... To the north, hill after hill, with bald top rising above the stunted trees on its sides, limited our range of vision. Far away to the south stretched a rolling, wooded country. To the eastward the country was flatter, with irregular ranges of low hills, all covered with a thick growth of spruce and fir balsam.

— Dillon Wallace, *Lure of the Labrador Wild*

It is hard to comprehend the size of Labrador unless you compare it to something familiar. It is possible to fit the whole of Great Britain into Labrador's area (294,330 km^2 (113,641 mi.^{2})) and have enough room left over for Denmark!

Referred to by early travellers as "The land that God gave Cain'" its beauty and ruggedness is hard to describe. To the north lie the Torngat Mountains, reaching skyward to 1,372 m (4500 ft.) and then plunging to the depths of the Labrador Sea. The central region is dominated by a plateau scoured by the last glacier 10,000 years ago. Its majestic wilderness encompasses 4 main vegetation zones and 10 ecoregions. The southernmost portion of Labrador is open mixed forest, which thins out to coniferous forest in central Labrador and gives way to the area of stunted open woodland at the edge of the tundra. Northern Labrador is tundra.

Deep fjords, especially in the area north of Nain, reach far inland like fingers trying to grasp the central plateau. The largest man-made mark is the Smallwood Reservoir located in the western area which supplies power to southern Canada and the eastern United States.

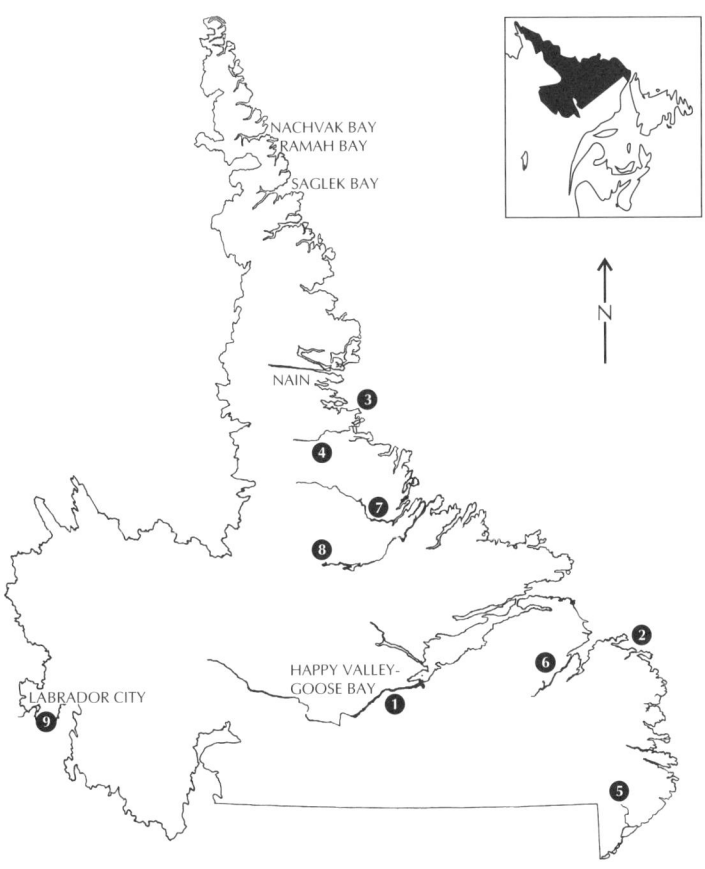

NACHVAK BAY
RAMAH BAY

SAGLEK BAY

NAIN

HAPPY VALLEY-
GOOSE BAY

LABRADOR CITY

1	Churchill River	6	Eagle River
2	Cartwright to Black Tickle	7	Ugjoktok River
3	Port Manverse Run - Nain Bay Loop	8	Kanairiktok River
4	Notakwanon River	9	Moisie River
5	Pinware River		

Churchill River

RAPIDS: Class 1-6.

WATER NOTES: This is a dam-controlled, high volume river with flow rates up to 60,000 m³ per second (cms). Downriver, channels are usually clear, but avoiding big water (waves) is essential to decrease the risk of swamping. In the event of a swamp or capsize, rescues must be quick and efficient to avoid a long swim.

DISTANCE: ○ Churchill Falls to Muskrat Falls - 400 km (250 mi.);

○ Churchill Falls to Goose Bay - 450 km (280 mi.).

DURATION: 6-9 days (add one day if you are paddling to Goose Bay).

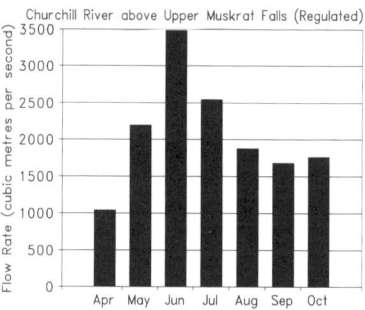

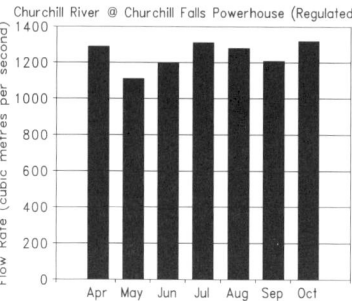

DESCRIPTION: The Churchill River, formerly the Hamilton River, is the longest river in Newfoundland and Labrador and also has the largest average discharge (1,900 cubic metres per second). Churchill Falls itself is the hydroelectric site (over 5,000 MW) which expanded the river's drainage area to almost 100,000 km² (38,610 mi.³) and transformed a spectacular falls to a mere trickle.

For the paddler, the trip begins just below the outflow of the power plant and stretches some 400 km (249 mi.) before you even have to think about a portage. To make it even better, the predominant westerly wind is at your back. The wildlife includes wolf, red fox, black bear, moose, numerous birds including Canada geese and some 20 different species of fish. There may be a rare sighting of a low flying F-16 since Goose Bay is NATO's low level flight training centre.

Your ability to ride the waves (line-her-up-and-go style) will be the determining factor in what you run and what you do not. Whatever we chose not to run, we lined on river left. The only two places we lined were Minipi Rapid (a very short stretch) and Gull Island Rapid. In both cases, they were probably runnable but in the interest of the group it was decided to line, since a swim would be a very long one. People have been known to swim for 3 km (2 mi.) after swamping in Gull Island Rapid. The current in the river is very fast and the river valley has few obstructions to pull into. Just above Muni Rapid is the "Devil's Elbow," which is a whirlpool that will spin your boat like a giant merry-go-round. The difficulty here to far river right is the giant whirlpool and to far river left are the biggest waves of the rapid which rebound off the left bank of the river (a challenging rapid no matter which way you go). It was in the waves that we had the first swamp of the trip. We were looking and laughing at the canoe in the whirlpool, then it was splash, splash, splash...swamp. Rescues with loaded boats in the fast current are difficult. We found joining rescue boats with throw bags and running with the current to shore, then "penduluming" the whole lot in, the fastest and simplest. Necessity was the mother of invention in this case.

Trips are made of memories and it sure helps when the paddlers of a new prospector canoe do not see the Volkswagen-sized rock in the middle of the rapid, flip over, have a swim, then a good hardy laugh—a humble reminder that it is nicer to paddle with those who are happy, fun loving and easy to rescue. In places along the river, fish surface like mini porpoises on top of the water. Much of the shoreline is sand and coniferous forest. Narrow bands of deciduous trees trace the path of brooks as they run from the highlands towards the river. In places, even in July, you will find mounds of snow covered with a thin layer of silt.

Experiencing a magnificent river like the Churchill makes it become more a part of you. When two hydro projects are planned for the river, you feel a personal loss. If everyone could experience the Churchill as wee did, it would be kept forever. At the mouth of Winokapau Lake on a breathless evening, we heard the wolves howl. We paddled alongside a curious black bear only 3 m (20 ft.) away on shore. The sun shone on one side of the river, thunder and lightning occurred on the other and, later that evening, a full rainbow bridged both sides of the river.

LOGISTICS: Take Route 340 north of the Trans Canada Highway at the Notre Dame Junction to Lewisport, where the ferry departs for Goose Bay (about 35 hrs). From Goose Bay, it is best to arrange with someone local to get to Churchill Falls. An 8 hour drive on a dirt road (use at your own risk) prone to washouts and delays will bring you to the community of Churchill Falls. These arrangements should be made well in advance. Choosing to fly is expensive and requires that you ship your gear so that it is there when you arrive.

MAPS: 23/H9, 13E/5, 13E/6, 13E/3, 13E/2, 13E/1, 13D/16, 13C/13, 13C/14, 13F/3, 13F/2, 13F/7, 13F/8.

CHART: N/A.

Hanging fog on the Churchill.

Cartwright to Black Tickle

RAPIDS: N/A.

WATER NOTES: Many of the islands on the 1:250,000 maps look navigable on the inside, but they are not, especially at low tide. Check your charts carefully before you try that shortcut. This also holds true for many of the small communities along the coast. Some of them are either abandoned or non-existent.

DISTANCE: 200 km (124 mi.).

DURATION: 8-10 days.

DESCRIPTION: When the great Canadian explorer, Vilhjalmur Stefansson, was asked if he had any adventures on his last expedition, he replied "an adventure only happens when you make a mistake." We do not know how many mistakes we made on this trip, but we did have more than our share of adventure. This trip to the rugged and exposed coast of Labrador also taught us great respect for "Murphy's Law"—if there is anything that can go wrong , it most certainly will when you least expect it.

There's a long list of incidents on this trip, but we will only share one with you now and maybe around a campfire some time, we will tell you the rest.

As if not to let us off lightly, on the second last day of the trip, the second storm hit. This time it was a little more than we had bargained for. At noon, we were driven ashore by a howling north wind, chilled by a thousand icebergs dotting the horizon. Here, on a narrow spit of land between the exposed Labrador Sea and a freshwater pond , we were pinned for 17 hours. One hundred and thirty km/hr (81 mi./hr.) winds battered our make-shift shelter as salt spray rained over us during high tide. The only high point of the day was at 4:00 AM when out of my pack, I pulled a flask of "Screech"(Nfld black rum) and made hot toddies for everyone to celebrate; it was my birthday.

Our "shelter" here was no more than half the bottom of a small fishing boat, approximately 4 m (13 ft.) long. We had propped up the splintered wreck when we landed, never thinking that the group would be huddled behind it until 5:00 AM the next morning when the wind died down enough to pitch a tent. At that point, 5 cold and tired souls dove into the 3 man tent, squirmed inside their sleeping bags and made themselves as comfortable as possible. Weighted down by 5 huge boulders and 5 bodies, all inside, we all prayed that the dome tent would not fly. As with our other shelter, this one withstood the conditions. We slept soundly until noon when the absense of wind made all of us stir.

Although not as striking as northern Labrador, the south coast offers an array of clear pools, islands, coves, tickles, bights, capes and channels, all of which invite exploration. Most of the coast is rolling, tundra-like terrain with some exposed bedrock. There are thick forests, but one has to paddle many kilometres up long bays to get to the river valleys where the vegetation is protected from the harsh Labrador climate.

Most of the wildlife along the coast is in the air or sitting on the water. You will see eider ducks, black ducks, razor bills, Canada geese and, if you are lucky, the endangered Peregrine Falcon. These birds, along with many others, can be seen in great numbers, especially in Table Bay which has recently been designated a bird sanctuary. Seals are also common but they are wary of humans.

LOGISTICS: Commercial airline flights are available to Goose Bay, Labrador. Regular scheduled flights travel from Goose Bay to Cartwright and Black Tickle via Air Labrador. There is a car ferry which runs from Lewisporte, Newfoundland to Cartwright, Labrador, or you can travel to almost any community with your boats and equipment by coastal boat. The latter can be time consuming and somewhat undependable because of weather and ice conditions. Contact Marine Atlantic for up-to-date schedules.

MAP: N/A.

CHARTS: 4732 (or 5138, 4712 and 5133).

Shelter from the Labrador gale.

An enjoyable voyage!

Port Manverse Run - Nain Bay Loop

RAPIDS: Class 1 rapids may be encountered in the more narrow sections of Port Manverse Run during the peak tidal flows.

WATER NOTES: Tidal currents flow from the north and south through Port Manverse Run to flood Web Bay and then reverse. Check your tide tables carefully to make sure you are travelling with the tide, or you could find yourself battling a 6 knot current.

DISTANCE: 190 km (9118 mi.).

DURATION: 8-10 days.

DESCRIPTION: Following the Twin Otter Labrador Air flight from Goose Bay to Nain (an adventure in itself), you can start your sea kayak trip right next to the landing strip which protrudes out into the harbour. Help in launching is not a problem, as the inquisitive nature of the local residents brings out many onlookers to see these funny looking people in these tiny boats. It is surprising how the use of kayaks as a means of transportation and hunting has virtually disappeared on the Labrador coast. From Nain, you head north through beautiful Port Manverse Run, a river-like body of water stretching 50 km (31 mi.) to Village Bay at the base of Mount Thoresby. This mountain rises 1,000 m (3280 ft.) straight out of the cold Labrador sea. If you catch the tide right, you can ride the 6 knot current, do eddy turns and surf the standing waves throughout much of the Run. If you do not, it is an uphill battle all the way.

Once you leave Village Bay, you are on the exposed Labrador coast—a sobering experience. From here, you have a choice of extending your trip by heading north along the majestic Kiglapait (sawtooth) Mountains. This would, however, require a full day of paddling along a coast, fully exposed to the open sea, with few landing zones and strong gusty winds rushing down from the mountains.

For those looking for a "tamer" wilderness experience, it would be best to head south and weave your way through the many uninhabited islands which make up the Nain Bay archipelago. The scenic beauty and tranquillity of these islands makes for excellent campsites; because of the strong historical native presence and very low population density, such campsites might even provide the opportunity to discover, as yet, hidden archaeological sites. Before ending the trip, a hike on Hillsbury or Paul Island is a rewarding experience. From the top of the 500 m (1600 ft.) cliffs, you have a delightful panoramic view of the entire Nain Bay area, including the community of Nain, which is less than a day's paddle away.

LOGISTICS: Commercial airline flights are available to Goose Bay, Labrador, with regular scheduled flights from Goose Bay to Nain via Air Labrador. You can also travel to Nain with your boats and equipment by ferry and coastal boat but this option requires considerable time and, due to unpredictable weather and ice conditions, is somewhat undependable.

MAPS: 14C/11, 14C/12, 14C/13, 14C/14.

CHARTS: 4775 or 4748 and 4763.

Notakwanon River

RAPIDS: Mostly Class 2 and 3 with some Class 4 and 5 at high water. Large standing waves are the determining factor of runnability along much of the river.

WATER NOTES: Surprisingly, few portages are required to descend the Notakwanon, but this number depends on the discretion or valour of the particular party. Five portages normally get you around the most serious obstructions, 4 being short and 1 portage over a kilometre long (0.6 mi.) around a beautiful waterfall.

DISTANCE: From the headwaters to the mouth of the river - 160 km (99 mi.).

DURATION: 6-10 days.

DESCRIPTION: Rarely does nature conspire to create a river solely for the pleasure of wilderness canoeists. The Notakwanon has superb whitewater canoeing, wildlife, beautiful scenery and total isolation, all pulled together along this 1 river corridor. Seemingly, the attempt is to fulfill all the demands of a total wilderness experience.

The Notakwanon does not cater in the slightest to the inexperienced wilderness traveller. Experts only should attempt the whitewater that often verges on the upper limit of open canoe paddling. The river trip requires significant physical stamina and a tolerance to foul weather and insects. Considerable time is spent scouting rapids and a mid-channel course is often impossible because of large standing waves. Dodging and lining is required along much of the boulder-strewn river banks. Kayaks, however, because of their nimble personality, can eddy-hop almost all of the river along with riding out much of the heavy water encountered in the mid-channel runs.

LOGISTICS: Float planes are the only convenient way to access the headwaters of the Notakwanon. The flight from Goose Bay to the headwater lake is 304 km (189 mi.). Take-out can be at either the mouth of the river at Merrifield Bay, which involves a pick-up by prearranged charter float plane, or an 85 km (53 mi.) saltwater paddle to the settlement of Nain, the most northerly community in Labrador. From Nain you can either fly back to Goose Bay by a regular scheduled commercial flight or you can catch a Marine Atlantic coastal boat that will return parties and equipment to Goose Bay or designated points in Newfoundland. Whichever choice is selected, allowances should be made for the possibility of being stormbound either at the mouth of the river or on the saltwater paddle to Nain.

MAPS: N.T.S. Map Scale 1:250,000 13M, 13N, 14C.

CHART: N/A.

A "must" portage on the Notakwanon.

Pinware River

RAPIDS: Class 1-5.

WATER NOTES: This river can be paddled during most of the paddling season. Its canyon (or "V") shape, endless obstacles and fast current make the Pinware a delight for the highly-skilled paddler. In low water, the section from the bridge to the park provides a pleasant mix of rapids and steadies for the paddler with reasonable skills in Class 2 rapids.

DISTANCE: ○ Country Cat Brook to bridge - 10 km (6 mi.);

              ○ bridge to Pinware River Provincial Park - 10 km (6 mi.);

              ○ Country Cat to Pinware Park - 20 km (12 mi.).

DURATION: 1-2 days.

DESCRIPTION: This river is traditionally known for its salmon fishing and black flies, yet it is a great canoe or kayak run. Because of the remoteness of the region there are only 3 known descents of this river: the first in a kayak, the second in a solo canoe, and, most recently, in a tandem canoe.

Of all the rivers in Labrador, the Pinware is one of the easiest to access by car. The drive along the Southern Labrador coast is scenic and diverse. Icebergs often drift past the large, sandy beaches, tall vertical rock faces and rolling treeless barrens that are typical of Labrador's Southern coastline. Where the highway meets the mouth of the Pinware River, the road turns inland and parallels the river making most rapids easy to survey.

The section of the river from Country Cat Pond to the bridge can be divided into 2 sections: above the shoot which consists primarily of a rock garden and below the shoot which is more drop and pool. An August trip usually offers moderately low water levels making the rock garden enjoyable, but the drops below the shoot manageable in an open boat. All sections of the river can be run in a kayak at any water level.

Shortly after starting at Country Cat Pond, there is a challenging water slide which drops about 3-4 m (10-12 ft.) at a 45° angle. The solo canoe is ideal for the tight turns of the rock garden.

After portaging the chute, quite probably runnable in a kayak, the river is faster, flowing with bigger water. There are 5 or 6 really nice runs in this section, Class 2-4. Some of the holes are much bigger than they appear. This section of the river is not boring, to say the least. What makes this run more interesting is the salmon fisherman and fishing guides watching and chasing the boats down the river, many of whom have never before seen a canoe in white water. Nimble on their feet they run, hop and dance along the shoreline, trying to keep up to catch all the action.

The take-out at the bridge is a 30 m (100 ft.) vertical portage. Another option is to stop traffic and pull the canoes up with a rope.

Below the bridge is an easy run, with Class 2 rapid being the most difficult. After this, the river begins to widen and becomes more shallow. As you near the ocean or park, the current begins to slow and the riverbanks change from rock to sand. If you are going to overnight on the river, the best place to camp would be just below the chute on river right. It is not a 5 star campsite, but it is a great place for fishing.

LOGISTICS: Take Route 510 about 20 km (12 mi.) north of the community of Pinware. When the river on your left side comes close to the level of the road and is not foaming white, it is as good a place as any to start. Take-out is at the bridge half way down or at the Provincial park at the end of the river (a nice place for a base camp). About 20 km (12 mi.) past the put-in is the national historic site of Red Bay: the Basque whalers' summer land base.

MAPS: 12P/10 , 13A/1, 12P/15.

CHART: N/A.

Looking north from Pinware Bridge.

Eagle River

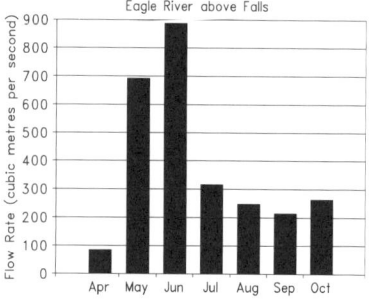

Eagle River above Falls

RAPIDS: Most of the rapids range from Class 1-3. You will encounter Class 4 and 5 if you decide to run the section known as "Devil's Gap," or if the water is high.

WATER NOTES: Because this is a big volume river, it is best run at low water. This, however, causes some difficulty in the lower sections of the river where selecting the proper channel becomes important and where the wrong choice may mean long stretches of lining and hauling.

DISTANCE: Park Lake to Sandwich Bay - 167 km (104 mi.).

DURATION: 5-7 days.

DESCRIPTION: My first introduction to the Eagle was an amusing one which happened in the early 1970s when I was working with the Forestry Department. We were setting up camp several hundred metres down river from a long steady in the river, the only place where a float plane could land. After unloading a ton of gear from the Beaver aircraft, we proceeded to carry the food and equipment down to the campsite. This went on for about half an hour, until someone noticed, among the gear, a rolled up 3 m (10 ft.) raft bought at some local hardware or sporting store.

With the help of the enclosed foot pump, it was quickly inflated, put into the river and loaded with the remainder of food and equipment. The lightest and most agile member of our group was then perched on top of this mountain of gear with a short paddle and instructed to guide the rubber dingy down several snarly rapids to the campsite. As a safety precaution, a rope was tied to the rig and the whole contraption was pushed out into the swift current. The raft accelerated down the glassy tongue and hit the first standing wave. No one had seen the razor sharp rock lurking beneath the surface and with a zipper-like sound, the floor of the raft was lanced from bow to stern. In only a few seconds, the mountain of gear disappeared and what was once sitting on the floor of the raft was now sitting on the floor of the river. Very little of the gear was recovered and replacements had to be flown in the next day (which was then carried down to the camp). As for the lone crew member, he was unceremoniously hauled ashore with what was left of our first "Self Bailing" raft.

The Eagle River is a demanding trip both in terms of canoe handling and the physical stamina required. Boulder gardens, bedrock ledges and a powerful whitewater canyon are the character of rapids found along the Eagle. Relatively few portages are required over the length of the trip. However, a considerable amount of lining and scouting is necessary. Most of the portages are short, except for the one around "Devil's Gap" as it is locally known. This is an exhausting and frustrating fight through dense forest for approximately 6 km (4 mi.). Closed boats can negotiate much of this canyon at medium to low water; however, caution is advised.

Below Devil's Gap is one of the best fishing pools for Atlantic salmon in the world and the first signs of development. To the left of the pool is a fishing lodge, the first of 4 which will be seen as you pass through the lower accessible reaches of the river. The last falls, occasionally called "Big Falls", is another very popular and renowned fishing area. Follow the narrow channel to the right of the island to avoid the larger volume falls. This is the last real challenge before entering Sandwich Bay, the end of the trip.

LOGISTICS: Float plane is the only convenient access to the headwaters of the Eagle River. Flying time from Goose Bay to Park Lake is less than an hour; however, down time for bad weather should be built into the trip schedule. Egress can be by float plane from the mouth of the river, or you can paddle another 30 km (19 mi.) to the town of Cartwright. From there, Marine Atlantic coastal boats can be used for shipping and transportation north to Goose Bay or south to insular Newfoundland. You can also fly from Cartwright to Goose Bay and points beyond, providing you are willing to leave canoes behind for shipping at a later date.

MAPS: N.T.S. Map Scale 1:250,000 13B, 13G, 13H.

CHART: N/A.

Devil's Gap.

Ugjoktok River

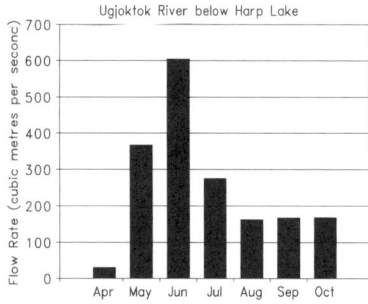

Ugjoktok River below Harp Lake

(Flow Rate - cubic metres per second)

RAPIDS: This river offers the full spectrum of white water from the calm stretches of the upper plateau to the Class 6 drops of the lower canyons.

WATER NOTES: Much more whitewater will be encountered than that which shows up on the topographical maps. High water in the many canyon sections would make lining impossible and increase the number of portages significantly.

DISTANCE: 160 km (99 mi.).

DURATION: 9-12 days.

DESCRIPTION: The Ugjoktok River begins east of the Labrador-Quebec border. From its headwaters (55°/15 minutes N 63°/15 minutes W), the river flows eastward within a deeply incised and sparsely vegetated valley. The region around the headwaters is an almost treeless and nearly perfect rock plain, free from all drift save isolated erratics. From these plains, the Ugjoktok passes into an area of tree-covered hills and sand plains. Near the coast is glacially-moulded hilly terrain with few striking features detectable from the river.

What is different about the Ugjoktok is that a side trip to Harp Lake half way down the river makes all the lining, hauling and portaging worthwhile. This lake is reached by tracking your canoe 10 km (6 mi.) up the Harp River. The scene at Harp Lake is awe-inspiring. Near the east end, rocky peaks rise more than 600 m (1900 ft.) above the fjord-like lake. A few kilometres down the lake, a sandy beach on the south shore provides a beautiful campsite. As another reward, the return trip down the river takes less than an hour, one third the time it took to track up.

The river can be divided into 5 separate sections, the first and last being the easiest to navigate. The middle 3 sections are filled with numerous falls, chutes, rapids and unrunnable canyons. Many of the portages are quite rigorous and require leaving the river and hiking along the ridge parallelling the valley. These portages range from less than 0.5 km (0.3 mi.) to over 1 km (0.6 mi.) in length and are over rough, difficult terrain. For expert kayakers, many of these canyons would be runnable, cutting down greatly on the number of portages.

LOGISTICS: Access to the starting point is by float plane, which can be chartered at Goose Bay. The termination is at the mouth of the Ugjoktok River, also by float plane.

MAPS: N.T.S. Map Scale 1:250,000 13M, 13N.

CHART: N/A.

Kanairiktok River

RAPIDS: Mostly Class 2 and 3, with chutes and falls. Probably some Class 4 at high water.

WATER NOTES: There are approximately 15 sets of rapids on the Kanairiktok, most of which can be run with scouting. Most of the portages are 500 m (0.3 mi.) or less, with 2 fairly difficult 1 km portages around waterfalls.

DISTANCE: The Kanairiktok river is 200 km (124 mi.) from Shipiskan Lake to the river mouth. The river's total length is approximately 320 km (200 mi.) from headwaters to the mouth.

DURATION: 10 days from Shipiskan Lake to Kanairiktok Bay with good weather— add a few days if journeying to Hopedale.

The Kanairiktok River is one of the few major rivers in central Labrador which connects the barrens and parkland of the interior with the Atlantic coast. In Inuktitut, the river's name means "the place with straight trees good for tent poles", while in Innumun, the river is known by at least 2 names, "Kainipeshiu-shipu" and "Ashtinekamuk". The latter name sounds somewhat similar to the English "Snegamook". Snegamook River was the name occasionally used by Euro-Canadians for the Kanairiktok in the early 20th century. However, Euro-Canadian cartographers chose to name the river for the coastal bay into which it flows. Aboriginal campsites along the river are a heritage resource protected by law. Recent Innu campsites in this Innu Nation land claim area must also be respected.

The river flows through some beautiful wilderness areas and the 2 waterfalls near its mouth are spectacular. The wilderness experience is periodically shattered when NATO warplanes are active in the low-level flying zone upriver from the east end of Snegamook Lake west to Shipiskan Lake. The jets are only occasionally seen and their overflights in that zone are usually limited to about an hour in the morning and in the afternoon, Monday to Saturday. Some canoeists would find this disturbance unacceptable. If so, begin your trip from Snegamook Lake's east end where the Kanairiktok River exits the lake.

You can begin at Shipiskan Lake, the outlet of the Shipiskan River and a major tributary of the Kanairiktok. During a helicopter overflight, it was clear that the Kanairiktok 10 km (6 mi.) upriver from Shipiskan Lake could be paddled, but above that, appeared to be a continuous rapid from the headwaters. Steep-sloping hills, considerably burnt over, surround both Shipiskan and Snegamook Lakes. One to 4 m (13 ft.) high sand dunes and terraces, largely tree-covered, are found at their south and east ends.

From Shipiskan Lake to Snegamook Lake, the river is generally broad and slow moving with numerous islands, having quite a bit of wildlife along its banks, especially moose and beaver. The landscape is one of rugged uplands and ranges of hills, with bare hilltops and ridges of sedimentary rock bordering a relatively narrow valley. The river flows through a broad estuary into Snegamook Lake, a 22 km (14 mi.) long waterbody subject to strong winds. Sandy beaches at the lake's east end make for good campsites. When paddling the lake, use caution and start early in the morning. Beware of the large southeast bay during a westerly wind as the waves pile up quickly.

Snegamook Lake to Kanairiktok Bay is the most challenging with about 12 rapids and 5 waterfalls. The rapids need to be scouted carefully and many mid-channel rocks often require you to hug the banks. Just below the major chute, approximately 20 km (12 mi.) east of the lake, there is a small cabin located on the southwest bank. This cabin is a federal hydrography station with sensitive equipment monitoring river flow. Fishing is good in the bay below the chute. Use extreme caution when approaching the 2 last falls near the river mouth at the head of Kanairiktok Bay. Here, you can arrange to be picked up by float plane or paddle this island-dotted section of the Labrador coast to Hopedale. If you are considering this coastal paddle, pay careful attention to tide tables and wind conditions.

LOGISTICS: Float plane or helicopter access will take you to Shipiskan or Snegamook Lakes, approximately 250 km (155 mi.) north of Goose Bay, Labrador. Take-out either at Kanairiktok Bay by float plane or helicopter, or an approximate 55 km (34 mi.) paddle to Hopedale on the Labrador coast. Regular passenger commercial flights connect Hopedale with Goose Bay. Passage can be booked at Hopedale on a Marine Atlantic freighter for Goose Bay or insular Newfoundland ports. Be prepared for weather delays regardless of transport choice.

MAPS: N.T.S. Map Scale 1:250,000 13L, 13K, 13F.

CHART: N/A.

H. Collins

Campsite on Long Steady.

Canyons, Coves and Coastal Waters

Mark Dykeman

Richard Banges (second from left), author and co-owner of Mountain Travel Sobeck savours the natural beauty of the Random Island Coast.

Bill Ritchie

"Reflections" in Cartwright, Labrador.

Jim Price

Giant Cirque: Kiglapait Harbour, Labrador.

Jim Price

Tranquility: a sunset on South Anlatsivik Island, Labrador.

Towering cliffs of Bell Island, Conception Bay.

Sunset in the Bay du Nord Wilderness Reserve.

Young canoeists en route to Hugh's Brook.

A warm and cozy end-of-day activity.

Moisie River

RAPIDS: Class 1-6.

WATER NOTES: N/A.

DISTANCE: 450 km.

DURATION: 14-21 days.

DESCRIPTION: Often referred to as the Nahani of the East, this majestic river offers just about every challenge and reward a wilderness paddler is looking for.

For those who live outside Labrador City, getting to the put-in of the Moisie is a trip in itself, highlighted by a 1-day train ride from Sept-Isles to Lac de Mille (25 km (16 mi.) south of Labrador City) where the paddling part of the trip begins.

The first 100 km (62 mi.) of the journey consists of a series of large lakes linked together by small to medium-sized paddlable rivers. In places, the wildlife seems undaunted with the paddler's presence. Imagine a still lake early in the morning. The call of the loon breaks the silence as a canoe slips quietly through the placid lake and then a muskrat carrying a fresh alder branch in its teeth swims within a paddle's length of the canoe. This is a typical scene in the headwaters of the Moisie.

Where the headwaters flow into the Moisie, the lakes' quiet serenity changes to a ceaseless roar of rapids and falls. This is the most arduous part of the trip as the portages are frequent and long. The hard work of portaging brings with it mixed blessings. No paddler loves to portage, yet the portage routes often force the paddler to go to places that offer scenic views and special rewards. One such place is the portage trail opposite the confluence of the Moisie and the Pekans Rivers. Here, golden sand lies beneath a stand of tall, symetric spruce trees 20-30 m (60-100 ft.) tall. Ripe bakeapples are scattered along the portage trail to quench your thirst and will leave you with a taste to remember.

In the last 250 km (155 mi.) of the river, portages become easier and less frequent. As the deep winding river valley collects more water, the river becomes wider, creating a greater variety of channels and more opportunities to line rather than to portage. On one occasion after portaging one canoe over and around house size boulders, we decided to line the second canoe through the Class 4 rapid. With 60 m (200 ft.) of rope on the stern line it came up short, letting go of the rope, the canoe dropped in the hole and washed out after a few tense seconds. Fortunately, the portaged canoe allowed for retreival of the lost canoe. With the wider river and a variety of channels, paddling 6 km of continous rapids including 900 m (3000 ft.) of Class 3 rapids is not uncommon. It is amazing in stretches like this how quickly you forget about the bugs and portages you encounter to get this far.

The Moisie is known as one of the best salmon rivers in North America with fish running up to 20-23 kg (45-50 lbs.). For many paddlers who enjoy to fish, the Moisie has it all. Train Tressle Rapid, the last rapid on the river, can be originally scouted from the train on your way to the put-in of the trip. Somehow, perception of the rapid changes when you are 30 m (100 ft.) closer and 2 weeks have passed. Paddling this final rapid without incident can leave you with mixed feelings of joy and emptiness. It is bittersweet to successfully complete the trip and to have to leave this majestic river. For those who paddle the Moisie it will always remain "The Nahani of the East". Although you may leave the river, the river will never leave you. This eternal spirit now awaits those of you with a spirit of respect, challenge and adventure to match.

LOGISTICS: Park in Sept-Isles or the campground in the community of Moisie (the river finishes in the community of Moisie). Take the Quebec North Shore and Labrador Railway operated by the Iron Ore Company of Canada up to the east Opocopa stop and start paddling onward and downward. It is a great trip.

If you wish to fly in, any of the lakes are accessible. If you wish to avoid the heavy portaging, some pilots will land at the confluence of the Pekans and the Moisie.

MAPS: 23G/2, 23G/1, 23B/15, 23B/16, 23B/10, 23B/7, 23B/2, 22-0/15, 22-0/16, 22-0/9, 22-0/8, 22-0/1, 22J/16, 22J/9, 22J/8, 22J/1.

CHART: N/A.

End of a long portage, Comfort Cove.

Gorge 90 km (56 mi.) from finish of Moisie.

A wilderness trip never comes to an end. After tents are dried, canoes or kayaks repaired and equipment stored, there are still the memories. Images of golden curtains of mist being lifted from a peatbog at sunrise, water so smooth that you seem to fly your kayak between two worlds and cold mists biting into the tree-covered hills start the paddler daydreaming and then planning for the next experience. The end of one paddling trip is the beginning of the next.

The routes described in this guide represent only a small fraction of the potential canoe and kayak routes in Newfoundland and Labrador. Many rivers, especially in Labrador, have never been paddled before, and many coves and inlets with their hidden beaches and secret places remain untouched. After completing some of the routes described in this guide, take out your maps, "chart your course and go out and explore" the lakes, rivers and coastal waters of Newfoundland and Labrador.

If you have any comments or feedback on the route decriptions contained within this guide or have a favourite trip not included in this book that you would like considered for inclusion in the next edition, please contact us at the following address:

Jim Price
Box 17, Site 14, R.R. #2
Paradise, Newfoundland
Canada, A1L 1C2

Evening silhouette on Ninety-Nine Island Pond.

Appendix 1

Air Charter Companies

Air Northland
P.O. 307, Station "A"
Goose Bay, Labrador
A0P 1S0
Contact: Clyde House
Telephone: (709) 896-8049

AirSport Atlantic, Inc.
P.O. Box 3
Corner Brook, Newfoundland
A2H 6C3
Contact: Pierre Meagher
Telephone: (709) 686-2521
Fax: (709) 635-3901

Ashuanipi Aviation Limited
624 McParland Dr.
Labrador City
Telephone: (709) 944-2395

Canadian Helicopters Ltd.
P.O. Box 5188
St. John's, Newfoundland
A1C 5V5
Contact: Don Penny
Telephone: (709) 570-0700
          (709) 570-0727

Clarenville Aviation Ltd.
P.O. Box 287
Shoal Harbour, Newfoundland
A0C 2L0
Contact: Neil Pelley
Telephone: (709) 466-2802

Labrador Airways
Goose Bay, Labrador
Telephone: (709) 896-8113

Labrador Travel Air Ltd.
Charlottetown, Labrador
A0K 5Y0
Contact: Tony Powell
Hanger: (709) 949-0273
Fax: (709) 949-0293
After Hours: (709) 949-0214

Pine Ridge Air Charter Service
Site 3, Box 1, Terra Nova
Newfoundland A0C 1L0
Contact: David Holloway
Telephone: (709) 265-6431

Provincial Airlines
Box 9460, St. John's
Newfoundland A1A 2Y4
Telephone: (709) 576-1804

Springdale Aviation Ltd.
P.O. Box 126
Springdale, Newfoundland
A0J 1T0
Contact: Rick Adams
Telephone: (709) 673-3272
Fax: (709) 673-4146

Thorburn Aviation Ltd.
P.O. Box 213, Shoal Harbour
Newfoundland A0C 2L0
Contact: Gene Ploughman
Telephone: (709) 466-7823

Universal Helicopters
P.O. Box 9025, Station "B"
St. John's, Newfoundland
A1A 2X3
Contact: Mike
Telephone: (709) 576-4611

Outfitters

Drover's Labrador Adventures
P.O. Box 121, Labrador City,
Labrador, A2V 2K3
Contact: Alonzo Drover
Telephone: (709) 944-6947

Eastern Edge Outfitters Ltd.
P.O. Box 17, Site 14, R.R. # 2
Paradise, Newfoundland
A1L 1C2
Contact: Jim or Margie Price
Telephone: (709) 782-1465

Gander River Tours Ltd.
Dorman's Cove, Gander Bay,
Newfoundland, A0G 2G0
Contact: Dan Stiles
Appleton, Newfoundland
Telephone: (709) 679-2271
Office: (709) 676-2254
Contact: Terry Cusack
Gander, Newfoundland
Telephone: (709) 256-3252

Gros Morne Adventure Guides
c/o Eastern Brook Cabins
P.O. Box 101, Pasadena,
Newfoundland, A0L lK0
Contact: Sue Rendall or
Bob Hicks
Telephone: (709) 686-2241
　　　　　(709) 458-2722

Labrador Scenic Ltd.
P.O. Box 233
North West River
Labrador, Newfoundland
A0P 1M0
Contact: Barbara Kitowski
Telephone: (709) 497-8326

Minipi Wilderness Resort
Blizzard Corporation
P.O. Box 340, Station "B"
Happy Valley, Goose Bay
Labrador, A0P 1E0
Contact: Jack Cooper
Telephone: (709) 896-2891
Fax: (709) 896-9619

New Found Adventures Limited
General Delivery
Frenchman's Cove
Bay of Islands, Newfoundland
A0L 1E0
Contact: Ray Humber
Telephone: (709) 789-2809

Newfoundland-Labrador Ecotour Adventures
8 Virginia Place, St. John's,
Newfoundland, A1A 3G6
Contact: Gene Mercer
Telephone: (709) 754-5500

Nor'East Treks
P.O. Box 117, Clarenville,
Newfoundland, A0E 1J0
Contact: Bryan Durant
Telephone: (709) 466-2036
　　　　　(709) 466-2008

Ray's Lodge Ltd.
P.O. Box 31, Howley,
Newfoundland, A0K 3E0
Contact: Ray Broughton
Telephone: (709) 635-3628

River Run Outfitting & Tours
P.O. Box 1095, Lewisporte,
Newfoundland, A0G 3A0
Contact: Horace Lane
Telephone: (709) 535-8770

Sandy Lake Lodge
9 Judges Terrace
P.O. Box 556
Grand Falls-Windsor, Newfoundland
A2A 2J9
Contact: Bill Lynch
Telephone: (709) 489-4662

Marble Mountain Cabins
P.O. Box 63, Corner Brook
Newfoundland, A2H 6C3
Contact: Joe Dieles
Telephone: (709) 489-4662
Canoe/Kayak Sales and Rentals

Tasiujatsoak Wilderness Camp
Location: Northern Labrador
327 St. Patrick Street, Ottawa,
Ontario, K2N 5K6
Contact: Ches & Cathy Anderson
Telephone: (613) 789-3855
Fax: (613) 234-1991

Victoria Outfitters
6 Birmingham St., St. John's,
Newfoundland, A1E 5C8
Contact: Dave Evans
Telephone: (709) 745-1048

Stan Cook's Wilderness Canoeing
67 Circular Rd., St. John's,
Newfoundland, A1C 2Z4
Contact: Stan Cook
Telephone: (709) 726-5900

Wilderness Conservation & Survival
Thorburn Aviation Ltd.
P.O. Box 213, Shoal Harbour,
Newfoundland, A0C 2L0
Contact: Gene Ploughman
Telephone: (709) 466-7823

Appendix 3

Provincial Government Departments

1. Department of Tourism

2. Department of the Environment,
   Water Resources Division

3. Department of Fisheries and Agriculture

4. Department of Wildlife

NOTE: All government departments can
be contacted at the following address:

P.O. Box 8700, St. John's,
Newfoundland, A1B 4J6
Telephone: (709) 729-2553

5. Gros Morne National Park
   Box 130, Rocky Harbour,
   Newfoundland, A0K 4N0
   Telephone: (709) 458-2066

6. Terra Nova National Park
   Glovertown, Newfoundland
   A0G 2C0
   Telephone: (709) 533-2801

Canyons, Coves and Coastal Waters

How To Do A River Profile

Gradient - gradient is described in ft. per mi. (fpm) or m per km (mpk). Both figures measure a river's average decent over a given distance.

To calculate the gradient, you need the following information:
1. elevation of river at the put-in (ie. 1800 ft.);
2. elevation of river at the take-out (ie. 0 ft. sea level);
3. distance between put-in and take-out (ie. 30 miles).

The gradient formula is:

$$\frac{\text{elevation at put-in} - \text{elevation at take-out}}{\text{distance between put-in and take-out}}$$

Example: $\dfrac{1800 \text{ ft.} - 0 \text{ ft.}}{30 \text{ mi.}}$ The gradient of this section of river is 60 ft./mi.

Rapids occur where the river's gradient exceeds the average gradient of the river, or there are obstructions (ie. boulders) in the path of the water as it descends toward the sea. Therefore, a river which decends evenly over the length of the river will have long, consistent rapids, whereas a drop and pool river will tend to have short, intense rapids. Generally, the higher the gradient, the more difficult the river.

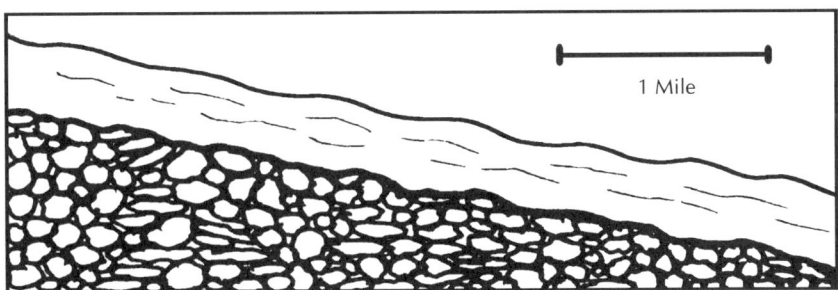

A continuous river.

A pool-drop river.

— Jeff Bennett, *Rafting: The Complete Guide To Whitewater Rafting.*

Resource List

Books

1. *Path of the Paddle: An Illustrated Guide to the Art of Canoeing*
   Bill Mason
   1980, Key Porter Books
   ISBN 0-919493-38-6

2. *Song of the Paddle: An Illustrated Guide to Wilderness Camping*
   Bill Mason
   Key Porter Books
   ISBN 1-55013-082-X

3. *Voyages: Canada's Heritage Rivers*
   Lynn Noel (ed.)
   1994, Breakwater Books
   ISBN 1-55081-099-5

4. *The Lure of the Labrador Wild*
   Dillon Wallace
   1983, Breakwater Books
   ISBN 0-919948-38-3

5. *Coastal Labrador*
   A Northern Odyssey
   Tony Oppersdorff
   Nimbus Publishing
   Halifax, Nova Scotia
   ISBN 0-921054-84-X

6. *River Rescue*
   Les Bechdel and Slim Ray
   1989, Appalachian
   Mountain Club Books
   5 Joy Street
   Boston, Mass.

7. *Guide to Sea Kayaking*
   Second Edition
   Derek C. Hutchinson
   1990, The Globe Pequot Press
   Old Saybrook, Connecticut, USA

For a free catalogue of these books and more contact:
   Canadian Recreational Canoeing Assoc.
   P.O. Box 5000, 446 Main St. West
   Merrickville, Ontario
   Canada, K0G 1N0
   (519) 473-2109 / 641-1261
   After Sept. 1/96: (613) 269-2910

Maps and Atlases

1. *Atlas of Newfoundland and Labrador*
   Gary E. McManus &
   Clifford H. Wood
   1991, Breakwater Books
   ISBN 1-55081-000-6

2. Source Of All Canadian
   Topographic Maps
   Department of Natural
   Resources, Lands Branch
   Box 8700
   St. John's, Newfoundland

3. Source Of All Canadian
   Topographic Maps
   Canada Map Office
   615 Booth Street
   Ottawa, Ontario K1A 0E9
   Telephone: (613) 952-7000
   Fax: (613) 957-8861

4. *Water Resources Atlas of Newfoundland*
   Water Resources Division:
   Department of Environment and
   Lands, Government of Newfoundland and Labrador, 1992.

Charts

1. Hydro Graphic Chart Distribution
   Office
   Dept. of Fisheries & Oceans
   1675 Russell Road,
   P.O. Box 8080
   Ottawa, Ontario
   Canada, K1G 3H6
   Phone: (613) 998-4931
   Fax: (613) 998-1217

2. Campbell's Ships Supplies
   P.O. Box 274
   689 Water Street West
   St. John's, Newfoundland
   Canada, A1C 5J2
   Phone: (709) 726-6932
   Fax: (709) 739-9896

Ecoregions of Newfoundland and Labrador

The thrill of running a Class 3 rapid, paddling across a lake through a morning mist or navigating your sea kayak into a hidden cove is just one part of a paddling experience. Experiencing the natural environment, the Newfoundland culture and learning about the history of the land will add considerably to the enjoyment of the trip, thereby further enhancing one's paddling experience.

The inclusion of a short description of each of the ecoregions of Newfoundland and Labrador will aid you in becoming familiar with the natural environment that you will be travelling through. These ecoregion descriptions are not detailed and are only meant to provide you with a starting point for further research. An ecoregion is a large, mostly continuous area where the relationship between living organisms and their physical environment is basically the same. The province of Newfoundland and Labrador is divided into 19 ecoregions, 9 on the island and 10 in Labrador. Although we have not included paddling routes that allow you to experience every ecoregion in our beautiful province, many of the routes do pass through or near many of them. Seven of the 9 ecoregions on the island of Newfoundland and 7 of the 10 ecoregions of Labrador lie on or near a described route in this guide.

These ecoregion summaries may be used in a variety of ways, some of which are described below:

If your prime reason for paddling this land is to experience its many unique natural areas, then these brief descriptions of each ecoregion will provide a starting point for planning your trip. Selecting a route matching your paddling ability and one that passes through or near the region of interest is the first step. From here, you then select the appropriate maps and field guides and carry out any additional research that will ensure an enjoyable visit to the region.

By studying the ecoregions that you will be paddling through or near, you will get a better picture of the physical features, climate, vegetation and animal life that you will experience. This, in turn, will enable you to better prepare for the trip by selecting appropriate clothing for the anticipated climate and by becoming familiar with the plants and animals that you might encounter.

Newfoundland Ecoregion 1: Western Newfoundland Forest

Location:

- mainly along the west coast, south of the Great Northern Peninsula, including the Corner Brook area, Port au Port Peninsula, St. George's Bay, Codroy Valley, and Cape Anguille Mountains.
- deep river valleys of the south coast such as Bay d'Espoir and Facheux Bay.

Physical Features:

Topography: hilly to mountainous.

Elevation: sea level to 810 m (Lewis Hills).

Bedrock: acidic, with some serpentine and extensive limestone-type bedrock areas.

Climate:

- the most favorable climate of the province.
- summers are warm, winters are cold.
- the warmest valleys of the island occur in this ecoregion.
- precipitation: 1000 mm to less than 1200 mm annually
    - average snowfall is 2.0 m to 4.0 m at sea level, more at higher elevations.
- average daily temperatures:
    - February average: ⁻5 to ⁻8°C
    - July average: ⁺14 to ⁺16°C

Vegetation:

- heavily forested; the main tree species is balsam fir.
- balsam fir forest, with an understory of ferns and feathermoss, is the typical forest type.
- the small number of fires have had little effect on the forest.
- the main wetland types are plateau bogs (deep, flat-topped bogs) along the coast, and shallow, rich fens in the forested areas.
- the flora is very diverse. It contains plants typically found:
    - in northern alpine areas
    - in more southern areas of eastern Canada and the U.S.
    - only in the Gulf of St. Lawrence
    - only on the east and west coasts of North America (but not in the continental interior).
- black ash, showy lady slipper*, and mayflower* are found only (*or mainly) in this ecoregion.
- several tree species have their northern limit in this ecoregion. These are:
    - yellow birch
    - red maple
    - white pine
    - trembling aspen

Animals:

- the main population of pine marten is located in the Grand Lake area.

Newfoundland Ecoregion 2: Central Newfoundland Forest

Location:

- ❍ primarily the north-central part of the island, including the Exploits and Gander River valleys, the Red Indian Lake area, and the Annieopsquotch Mountains.
- ❍ the upper part of the Bay d'Espoir valley.

Physical Features:

Topography:	gently rolling to hilly.
Elevation:	mostly between 150 m and 450 m.
	Annieopsquotch Mountains have elevations to 677 m.
Bedrock:	mainly acidic.

Climate:

- ❍ this region has the most continental climate on the island, with the warmest summers and coldest winters, and the least wind and fog.
- ❍ warm summers and high rates of evapo-transpiration make this one of the driest areas of the island, with reference to soil moisture.
- ❍ precipitation: 900 mm to 1300 mm annually.
  - • average snowfall is about 3.0 to 3.5 m.
- ❍ average daily temperatures:
  - • February average: ⁻4 to ⁻8°C
  - • July average: ⁺15 to ⁺16°C

Vegetation:

- ❍ heavily forested; balsam fir and black spruce are the most important tree species.
- ❍ the typical forest type in areas not disturbed by fire is a balsam fir forest with a dense understory of feathermosses.
- ❍ frequent and extensive fires have created many black spruce and white birch fire stands in northern and eastern parts of the ecoregion.
- ❍ open black spruce forests with a dwarf shrub (mainly *Kalmia*) understory occur in areas which have been burned repeatedly.
- ❍ open black spruce forests with an understory of dwarf shrubs and lichens (caribou lichens) are found only in this ecoregion. They occur on very coarse soils (outwash sands and gravels) which are low in nutrients.
- ❍ the main wetland type is domed bog (bogs with a raised surface, highest in the centre) with concentric pool patterns.
- ❍ red pine is found mainly in this ecoregion, but only on extremely dry sites.
- ❍ yellow birch is absent; red maple occurs as a shrub throughout the region, but can grow to tree size only in eastern and northern areas of the ecoregion.

Animals:

- ❍ barren areas in this ecoregion are an important habitat for migrating caribou.

Newfoundland Ecoregion 3: North Shore Forest

Location:
- along the northeast coast, from the Bonavista to the Baie Verte Peninsulas.

Physical Features:

Topography: rolling to hilly; interrupted by many deep bays and inlets.

Elevation: most are less than 130 m

elevations reach about 315 m on the Baie Verte Peninsula.

Bedrock: mainly acidic.

Climate:
- the warmest summers of any *coastal region* in the province.
- although rainfall in this region is higher than in the Northern Peninsula, high summer temperatures and high winds from its exposed location cause high rates of evapo-transpiration, making this the driest part on the island, with respect to soil moisture.
- precipitation: 900 mm to 1200 mm annually
  - average snowfall is 2.5 m to 3.5 m.
- average daily temperatures:
  - February average: $^-$5 to $^-$7°C
  - July average: $^+$15 to $^+$16°C

Vegetation:
- mostly forest covered; black spruce and balsam fir are the most common tree species.
- forest fires occur regularly, so black spruce fire stands are common.
- high winds decrease the size of trees in forests near the coast.
- crowberry barrens occur on exposed headlands.
- domed bogs (deep bogs with a raised surface, highest at the centre), basin bogs (shallower, flat-topped bogs located in depressions) and shallow, rich fens are the most common wetland types.
- white spruce is more common, but trembling aspen is less common than in central Newfoundland.
- some northern species, usually found in coastal areas, will not grow in this ecoregion due to the high summer temperatures.

Animals:
- several seabird colonies occur on offshore islands.

Newfoundland Ecoregion 4: Northern Peninsula Forest

Location:

- ○ the forested areas and most of the coastal areas of the Great Northern Peninsula.

Physical Features:

Topography: flat to undulating in the west; hilly in the east.

Elevation: sea level to less than 200 m in the west to 450m in the east.

Bedrock: mainly acidic in the east; basic (limestone-type) bedrock is common in the west and north.

basic (serpentine) bedrock is found only in the White Hills near St. Anthony.

Climate:

- ○ summers are cool and short, winters are cold and long.
- ○ precipitation: 900 mm to 1000 mm annually
  - average snowfall is less than 3.0 m to 3.5 m.
- ○ average daily temperatures:
  - February average: $^-8$ to $^-13°C$
  - July average: $^+13$ to $^+15°C$

Vegetation:

- ○ the east coast and western valleys are heavily forested; balsam fir is the main tree species.
- ○ forest fires are infrequent, so black spruce stands are uncommon, except at higher elevations.
- ○ most common forest types are balsam fir with an understory of herb species.
- ○ low coastal areas in the west have extensive deep, flat-topped bogs; shallow, rich fens are common in areas with limestone bedrock.
- ○ crowberry and dwarf shrub (*Kalmia*) barrens are common along the east coast; limestone barrens occur on some west coastal areas.
- ○ due to the colder winter temperatures, cold winds, and lower precipitation, over 100 species of plants common throughout Newfoundland are absent from (or restricted to the extreme south of) this ecoregion. Tree species mainly absent from this ecoregion are:
  - yellow birch
  - red maple
  - white pine
  - trembling aspen

Animals:

- ○ seabird colonies occur on coastal islands.
- ○ common eider ducks are characteristic of this ecoregion. The Hare Bay Ecological Reserve provides a breeding habitat for this endangered bird species, whose population numbers have been drastically reduced due to overhunting. The Canadian Wildlife Service is presently restoring breeding populations of common eiders to this area.

Newfoundland Ecoregion 5: Avalon Forest

Location:
○ the sheltered, central, forested portion of the Avalon Peninsula.

Physical Features:

Topography: irregular with low steep-sided hills.

Elevation: below 250 m.

Bedrock: acidic, covered by ribbed moraine.

Climate:
○ the climate is similar to that of the surrounding Maritime Barrens, but this region is more sheltered because of its interior position.

○ summers are cool, winters are mild.

○ fog occurs frequently, brought into the area by the prevailing southerly winds.

○ precipitation: 1400 mm to 1500 mm annually.

- average snowfall is 2.0 m to 2.5 m.

○ average daily temperatures:

- February average: ⁻4 to ⁻7C

- July average: ⁺14 to ⁺16 C

○ the moraines (hills of coarse gravels deposited by glaciers) in this ecoregion have a unique microclimate:

- night frost occasionally hits south-facing slopes well into the summer, when northeast winds bring cold air into the area; however, air turbulence prevents this cold air from settling on north-facing slopes and hill tops. Thus, the upper north slopes and hill tops have higher temperatures and a longer growing season. This difference is reflected in the forest types growing on the hills.

Vegetation:
○ heavily forested; balsam fir and black spruce are the main tree species, yellow birch is also important.

○ the unique microclimate of the moraines, described above, produces a distinct vegetation pattern. The upper north slopes and hill tops typically have a forest of balsam fir and yellow birch with a thick understory of ferns. The colder lower north slopes have a poorer forest of balsam fir and black spruce, while the coldest south slopes have a scrubby forest of balsam fir and black spruce.

○ yellow birch is important only in this and the Western Newfoundland Ecoregion (1).

○ large amounts of tree lichens, commonly called old-man's beard, hang from the trees.

○ domed bogs (deep, bogs with a raised surface, highest in the centre) occur between hills.

Animals:
○ animals that prefer deciduous and mixed forest habitats are common.

Canyons, Coves and Coastal Waters

Newfoundland Ecoregion 6: Maritime Barrens

Location:

- most of the Avalon, Bonavista and Burin Peninsulas.
- the central barrens.
- the south, coastal area from the Burin Peninsula to Port aux Basques.

Physical Features:

Topography: rolling hills.

Elevation: from sea level to around 300 m.

Bedrock: mainly acidic.

Climate:

- summers are cool to cold, winters are mild.
- fog occurs frequently, less often inland.
- precipitation: 1250 mm to more than 1600 mm annually.
- winter precipitation may be either snow or rain:
  - a permanent winter snow cover occurs only on the interior barrens.
- average daily temperatures (lowest in inland areas):
  - February average: ⁻3 to ⁻8°C
  - July average: ⁺13 to ⁺16°C

Vegetation:

- frequent fires, mainly caused by man, have destroyed most of the previous forest cover.
- forest is common only in valleys that escaped fire; balsam fir is the most important tree species in these forests.
- dwarf shrub barrens (mainly *Kalmia*) now cover the extensive areas that were once forested.
- exposed sites with no snow cover have alpine barren with crowberry and partridgeberry instead of dwarf shrub (*Kalmia*) barren.
- slope bogs (shallow bogs on slopes), basin bogs (shallow, flat-topped bogs in depressions), and poor fens are the common wetland types.
- plant species usually found in northern alpine or arctic areas can be found in exposed alpine barrens.
- plant species usually found in more southern areas of eastern Canada and the U.S. can be found in bogs and valleys of this ecoregion.

Animals:

- major wintering grounds or year round ranges for several caribou herds occur in the central barrens.
- many seabird colonies occur on offshore islands. The most well known are protected in the Witless Bay Ecological Reserve. Storm petrels, puffins, kittiwakes, herring gulls, and murres breed on islands in this reserve.

Newfoundland Ecoregion 7: Eastern Hyper-oceanic Barrens

Location:

- ○ the southernmost parts of the Avalon and Burin Peninsulas.
- ○ the extreme coastal areas of Bay de Verde and Cape Freels.
- ○ offshore islands such as Baccalieu, Funk, and Wadham Islands.

Physical Features:

Topography: flat to rolling.
Elevation: sea level to about 200 m.
Bedrock: mainly acidic.

Climate:

- ○ the most oceanic climate in the province.
- ○ summers are very cool and winters are mild.
- ○ fog occurs frequently and is persistent.
- ○ precipitation: 1250 mm to nearly 1450 mm; less than 1000 mm at Cape Freels
  - • average snowfall is 2.0 m to 2.5 m.
  - • snow cover is less persistent than in any other part of the island due to the milder temperatures.
- ○ average daily temperatures:
  - • February average: ⁻3 to ⁻5°C
  - • July average: ⁺12 to ⁺14°C

Vegetation:

- ○ due to the extreme exposure, forests grow only as scattered pockets of stunted tuckamoor (tuck); balsam fir is the most common tree species.
- ○ coastal barrens and shallow, blanket bogs (shallow bogs that cover very large areas) are the most common and most extensive vegetation types; blanket bogs are characteristic of this region.
- ○ plant species usually found in more southern areas of eastern Canada and the U.S. can be found in the same habitats as plant species usually found in northern arctic or alpine areas. This is the only ecoregion where these two very different types of plants can be found in the same habitat.

Animals:

- ○ the largest seabird colonies in the province occur in this region, including Funk Island, Baccalieu Island, Cape St. Mary's.
- ○ the largest numbers of the rare harlequin duck winter near Cape St. Mary's.

Newfoundland Ecoregion 8: Long Range Barrens

Location:

○ this ecoregion is composed of 3 highland areas separated by continuous forest.

○ the northern subregion includes the northern portion of Long Range Mountains and the Highlands of St. John.

○ the central subregion includes that portion of the southern Long Range Mountains east of Grand Lake, including the Buchans Plateau and the Topsails.

○ the southern subregion includes that portion of the southern Long Range Mountains nearest the south coast.

Physical Features:

Topography:	mountainous highlands and plateaus.
Elevation:	200 m to over 650 m.
Bedrock:	mainly acidic.

Climate:

○ summers are cool, winters are cold.

○ this region includes the coldest area of the island (the Highlands of St. John).

○ precipitation: northern subregion:1000 mm to 1150 mm
  central subregion:1000 mm to 1300 mm
  southern subregion:1250 mm to 1600 mm

  • average snowfall varies from 3.0 to over 4.0 m, but can be greater than 5 m.

  • winter snow cover ispersistent until late spring; drifting is extreme.

○ average daily temperatures:

  • February average:$^-$5 to $^-$8°C

  • July average:$^+$13 to $^+$15°C

Vegetation:

○ most of this ecoregion is barren, but unlike the Maritime Barrens Ecoregion, fire was of little importance in its development.

○ slopes and less sheltered valleys have extensive areas of black spruce tuck, only deep sheltered valleys have balsam fir forest.

○ dwarf shrub (*Kalmia*) barrens cover large areas and are the main vegetation.

○ crowberry barrens grow on exposed areas.

○ extensive, but shallow, slope bogs and shallow, ribbed fens are the common wetland types.

○ snowbed plants are characteristic of the northern subregion, where snow is most persistent.

○ plant species usually found in northern and arctic areas are common in this ecoregion; but species more typical of southern areas are absent in all areas except in deep river valleys along the south.

Animals:

○ two major caribou herds occur in this region.

○ arctic hare is found mainly in this ecoregion of the island.

Newfoundland Ecoregion 9: Strait of Belle Isle Barrens

Location:
○ the northernmost part of the Great Northern Peninsula.

Physical Features:

Topography: flat and rocky along the west coast; hilly in the east.

Elevation: mostly below 60 m.

Bedrock: mainly limestone-type bedrock in the west; acidic bedrock in the east.

Climate:
○ summers are short and cool, winters are long and cold.
○ the lowest summer and average annual temperatures in the island occur in this ecoregion.
○ pack ice, which persists off the coast until mid-June, contributes to the low summer temperatures.
○ fog occurs frequently.
○ precipitation: 760 mm to 900 mm
  • average snowfall is between 2.5 and 3.0 m.
○ average daily temperatures:
  • February average: around $^-9°C$
  • July average: $^+12$ to $^+14°C$

Vegetation:
○ rocky, coastal barrens cover the entire region.
○ this area has the most tundra-like vegetation on the island.
○ trees (white spruce, black spruce and balsam fir), form only tuck.
○ "limestone" barrens are characteristic of the west coast of this ecoregion.
○ very rich fens occur in wet areas throughout the "limestone" barrens.
○ a unique and very diverse mixture of plant species are found in the "limestone" barrens. Among these are plants typically found only from:
  • the Gulf of St. Lawrence
  • the east and west coasts of North America
  • northern arctic areas
  • limestone areas

Animals:
○ the white-crowned sparrow, common in Labrador barrens, is found only in this ecoregion of the island. This is a reflection of the very cold conditions that occur in this region.

Labrador Ecoregion 1: Low Arctic Tundra - Cape Chidley

Location:
○ the northernmost tip of Labrador.

Physical Features:
Topography: flat to hilly.
Elevation: sea level to around 630 m.
Bedrock: mainly acidic.

Climate:
○ dry arctic climate; the driest in Labrador.
○ summers are short and cool, winters are long and very cold.
○ precipitation: 500 mm to 600 mm annually.

  • average snowfall is less than 3.0 m.
○ average daily temperatures:

  • February average: ⁻20 to ⁻22°C
  • July average: ⁺6 to⁺7°C

Vegetation:
○ mainly tundra: bare rock and soil with patches of moss and lichens.
○ grassy meadows occur in areas where snow collects.
○ true arctic species are common.
○ no tall shrubs or trees occur in this region.
○ no true peatlands occur; marshes may occur along rivers.

Animals:
○ true arctic mammal species, such as walrus, polar bear, and narwhal, are often found in this region.

Labrador Ecoregion 2: Low Arctic - Alpine Tundra - Torngat

Location:
- the Torngat Mountains in northern Labrador.

Physical Features:

Topography: mountainous, with deep valleys (fjords).

Elevation: to about 1670 m.

Bedrock: acidic.

Climate:
- moist arctic climate.
- summers are short and cool; winters are long and very cold.
- precipitation: 500 mm to 700 mm annually
  - average snowfall is 3.0 m.
- average daily temperatures:
  - February average: ⁻19 to lower than ⁻22°C
  - July average: ⁺7 to ⁺9°C

Vegetation:
- tundra, with much bare rock, covers the plateaus.
- grassy meadows with sedges and dwarf willow occur in areas where snow collects.
- alder and dwarf willow thickets grow on wet slopes and stable lower slopes.
- conifer trees are absent, but groves of white birch and balsam poplar can be found in some valleys.
- shallow fens and marshes occur along rivers.

Animals:
- the Torngat caribou herd roams over much of this region.
- musk ox have moved into this region from Quebec, where they were recently reintroduced.
- polar bears may den in coastal areas.

Canyons, Coves and Coastal Waters

Labrador Ecoregion 3: High Subarctic Tundra - Kingurutik/Fraser

Location:

○ the George River Plateau in the north.

○ southern mountain ranges, including the Benedict, Red Wine, and Mealy Mountains.

○ the McPhadyen Plateau in the west.

Physical Features:

Topography: high plateaus, cut by deep valleys in the north; mountainous in the isolated southern areas

Elevation: between 630 m to 1000 m.

Bedrock: acidic.

Climate:

○ subarctic, continental climate

○ summers are short and cool, winters are long and very cold.

○ precipitation: 700 mm to 1000 mm annually

  • average snowfall is 3.0 m to 4.0 m.

○ average daily temperatures:

  • February average: ⁻16 to lower than ⁻22°C

  • July average: ⁺9 to ⁺13°C

Vegetation:

○ tundra, with over 50% bare rock, occurs on the plateaus; valleys are forested.

○ a continuous cover of sedge meadow occurs in areas where snow collects.

○ tree limit is located at Napoktok Bay, the northern boundary of this ecoregion.

○ white birch and willows grow on upper slopes, forming a transition zone between tundra and the coniferous forest.

○ black spruce forests occur on mid and lower slopes.

○ open spruce forests with a lichen understory (lichen woodland) occupy river terraces. The main lichens are *Stereocaulon* species, rather than caribou lichens, which dominate further south.

○ shallow fens with frozen peat occur on the plateaus.

Animals:

○ this is the most important region in Labrador for caribou.

Labrador Ecoregion 4: Coastal Barrens - Okak/Battle Harbour

Location:

- ○ the coastal zone from Napoktok Bay (Black Duck Bay) south to the Strait of Belle Isle.

Physical Features:

Topography: hilly, with exposed headlands, sheltered bays and many offshore islands.

large river terraces with marine sediments are characteristic.

Elevation: sea level to 630 m.

Bedrock: acidic.

Climate:

- ○ subarctic climate
- ○ summers are cool to warm (in the south), winters are cold.
- ○ precipitation: 1000 mm to 1300 mm annually
  - • average snowfall is 3.0 m to 4.0 m.
- ○ average daily temperatures:
  - • February average: ⁻10 to ⁻19°C
  - • July average: ⁺9 to ⁺13°C

Vegetation:

- ○ crowberry barrens are the most common type of plant community on the headlands; sheltered valleys are forested.
- ○ spruce tuck, on upper slopes, forms a transition between crowberry barren and spruce forests.
- ○ continuous spruce forests, with a moss understory, occur on mid and lower valley slopes.
- ○ lichen woodlands occupy river terraces; the main lichens are the caribou lichens: *Cladina* species.
- ○ repeated fires have changed many previously forested areas to dwarf shrub barrens with Labrador tea, dwarf birch and alder.
- ○ plateau bogs (deep flat-topped bogs) and saltmarshes occur on river terraces.
- ○ basin bogs (shallow, flat-topped bogs in depressions) occur on headlands.

Animals:

- ○ seven major seabird breeding colonies are located on coastal islands, the largest is Gannet Clusters, which has puffins, murres, and razorbills.
- ○ several seal species bear their pups on offshore islands and coastal areas.
- ○ the Mealy Mountain caribou herd winters on the southern shore and islands of Groswater Bay.

Labrador Ecoregion 5: Mid Subarctic Forest - Michikamau

Location:
○ the upland plateaus of central and western Labrador.

Physical Features:

Topography: flat to rolling plateaus.

Elevation: from around 330 m to over 500 m.

Bedrock: acidic; bedrock is covered by deep glacial tills and glacial deposits. These deposits (drumlins and eskers) are characteristic of this region.

Climate:
○ subarctic, continental climate.
○ summers are cool and short, winters are long, cold, and severe.
○ precipitation: 900 mm to 1000 mm annually
  • average snowfall is 3.5 m to 4.5 m.
○ average daily temperatures:
  • February average: ⁻17 to lower than ⁻22°C
  • July average: ⁺11 to ⁺13°C

Vegetation:
○ open lichen woodland is the main type of plant community on dry sites. It is not restricted to river terraces.
○ lichen woodlands have more tree and shrub cover here than southern lichen woodlands on river terraces.
○ frequent fires have increased the distribution of lichen woodland in this ecoregion.
○ black spruce is the most common tree species, except in northernmost portions of this ecoregion, where white spruce is more common. Larch is common on moist soils.
○ extensive, low, wet areas are covered with ribbed fens and string bogs and are surrounded by wet black spruce-bog forests with a sphagnum moss understory.
○ balsam fir is rare, trembling aspen does not occur north of this region, and the one known site for jack pine is south of Lake Ashuanipi.
○ ribbed fens are the most common and widespread wetland type.

Animals:
○ forest and wetland animals are more common than animal species preferring barren habitats.
○ fishers are invading forested river valleys in western regions.

Labrador Ecoregion 6: High Boreal Forest - Lake Melville

Location:
○ the Churchill River valley.
○ the Lake Melville area.

Physical Features:

Topography: rolling uplands and flat
coastal plain.

Elevation: sea level to 500 m.

Bedrock: acidic.

Climate:
○ boreal climate, the most favorable
climate in Labrador.
○ summers are warmer and winters are
shorter than in surrounding areas.
○ precipitation: 800 mm to 1000 mm annually.

  • average snowfall is 4.0 m.
○ average daily temperatures:

  • February average: ⁻14 to ⁻18°C

  • July average: ⁺13 to over ⁺14°C

Vegetation:

○ forest is the main type of vegetation; the most productive forests in Labrador
occur in this region.
○ balsam fir, white birch and trembling aspen are common on valley slopes.
Black spruce is the main tree species on upland areas and river terraces, where
fires are also most common.
○ black spruce lichen woodland occur on river terraces.
○ plateau bogs (deep, flat-topped bogs) occur along the shores of Lake Melville.
○ shallow fens are the common wetland type in upland depressions.

Animals:

○ several bird species typical of more southern areas of Canada are found only
in this part of Labrador.
○ bird and mammal species that prefer deciduous or mixed forests are common.
○ the largest number of amphibian species (4) in Labrador have been found in
this ecoregion:

  • two salamander species, one frog and one toad species can be found here.

Labrador Ecoregion 7: Mid Boreal Forest - Paradise River

Location:
○ southeastern Labrador.

Physical Features:
Topography: rolling.
Elevation: around 170 m to 500 m.
Bedrock: acidic.

Climate:
○ boreal climate, moister and cooler than the Lake Melville area.
○ summers are cool to warm, winters are short and cold.
○ precipitation: 1000 mm to over 1200 mm annually.
  • average snowfall is 4.0 m to 5.0 m.
○ average daily temperatures:
  • February average: ⁻12 to ⁻15°C
  • July average: ⁺12 to ⁺13°C

Vegetation:
○ fairly productive forests of black spruce and balsam fir are the main vegetation type.
○ fires have occurred frequently throughout the region.
○ after fire, white birch and aspen will dominate moist slopes, while lichen woodland will take over on well-drained sites.
○ domed bogs (deep bogs with a raised surface, highest in the centre) are characteristic of the valleys in this region.
○ string bogs and ribbed fens cover very large areas.

Animals:
○ birds and mammals that prefer deciduous forest habitats are common.

Labrador Ecoregion 8: Low Subarctic Forest - Mecatina River

Location:

○ mainly in southern Labrador.

○ two other, separate areas, one north of Lake Melville and the other north of the Red Wine Mountains, are part of this ecoregion.

Physical Features:

Topography: rolling hills and broad, flat river valleys.

Elevation: 500 m to 670 m.

Bedrock: mainly acidic, overlain by glacial deposits. shallow glacial till, drum-lins, and eskers are characteristic of this region.

Climate:

○ subarctic, continental climate.

○ summers are warm, winters are cold.

○ precipitation: less than 800 mm to 1300 mm annually.

   • average snowfall is 3.5 m to over 5.0 m.

○ average daily temperatures:
   February average: ⁻13 to ⁻21°C
   July average: around ⁺13°C

Vegetation:

○ black spruce forests with some balsam fir are the main type of vegetation.

○ lichen woodland occurs only on drier sites.

○ deciduous trees are not very common and white spruce is rare.

Animals:

○ forest, wetland and aquatic animal species are important in this region.

Labrador Ecoregion 9: String Bog - Eagle River Plateau

Location:

○ the Eagle River Plateau in southern Labrador.

Physical Features:

Topography: flat to rolling upland plateau.

Elevation: 500 m to 670 m.

Bedrock: acidic, a few eskers are
noticeable on the
wetlands.

Climate:

○ subarctic climate, less continental than that of Labrador ecoregions 5 and 8.

○ summers are cool, winters are cool to cold.

○ precipitation: 1000 mm to 1200 mm annually.

• average snowfall is 5.0 m.

○ average daily temperatures:

• February average: ⁻13 to ⁻16°C

• July average: around ⁺13°C

Vegetation:

○ extensive string bogs are the most common type of vegetation.

○ scrubby black spruce, Labrador tea, and feathermosses dominate raised areas and hummocks in the string bogs.

○ open lichen woodland occurs only on eskers or other glacial deposits.

○ alder swamps (thickets) are common along riverbanks.

Animals:

○ waterfowl and birds of prey are very important in this region.

Labrador Ecoregion 10: Forteau Barrens

Location:
- the most southeastern tip of Labrador, adjacent to the Strait of Belle Isle.

Physical Features:
Topography: low hills.

Elevation: sea level to 500 m.

Bedrock: mainly acidic, with some basic bedrock (limestone) in southern areas.

Climate:
- boreal climate.
- summers are cool and rainy, winters are fairly cold.
- precipitation: 1000 mm to 1250 mm annually
  - average snowfall is 3.5 m to 4.5 m.
- average daily temperatures:
  - February average: ⁻9 to ⁻12.5°C
  - July average: around ⁺12°C

Vegetation:
- barrens, with crowberry, alpine bilberry, and a thick lichen layer, cover much of this area.
- fire has probably played a part in the formation of the upland barren vegetation.
- most trees grow as scrubby tuck, due to the strong winds and wet soils.
- black spruce and larch will grow to normal tree heights only on well-drained slopes.
- slope bogs (shallow bogs located on slopes) are the most common type of wetland.

Animals:
- animal species that prefer barren or shrubby habitats are more common in this region.

Boils - surges of vertically rising water which produce confused and unpredictable currents on the surface.

Brace - the use of the paddle blade to give support or to recover from instability.

Broadside/Broach - running sideways onto an obstruction in the current, such as a rock.

Bulkhead - a solid material which separates the cockpit of the kayak from the storage compartments.

Dry suit - paddling suit worn over a layer of insulating clothing keeping it dry and therefore avoiding the loss of insulation. An experienced paddler's cold weather alternative to a wet suit.

Eddy - any area of slack or counter-moving water in the presence of the main flow.

Eddy Line - the line of water which separates the slack eddy water from the main current.

Ender or Backender - standing the canoe or kayak vertically.

Ferry - crossing the current so as not to lose ground downstream.

GPS - geographical positioning system.

Hatch - the opening which allows access to the storage compartments of the kayak.

Hatch Cover - the material which covers the hatch and prevents water from entering the storage compartment.

Haystack - a standing wave with a cascading peak.

Hole - a stopper created on the downstream side of a rock.

Hull - the underside of the canoe or kayak.

Hypothermia - a lowering of the body core temperature as a result of immersion, exhaustion or both.

Karabiner - a metal link to make quick connections with ropes and webbings.

Rips - are found in areas with gently sloping beaches and are caused by the water returning out to sea in deep water channels. Some rips may reach speeds of over 10 knots.

Sea Stack - a rock spire or column separated from the mainland by water. Sometimes they extend several hundred feet vertically in the air. They may occur singularly or in groups.

Seal Launch - launching off a bank or rock shelf after first getting in the kayak or canoe.

Sideslip - the sideways movement of a canoe or kayak across the water as the boat drifts downstream.

Snowmelt - the natural run-off of thawed snow which fills many rivers in spring. In the far north it can fill a river in summer. Glacial snowmelt will feed a river everyday throughout the summer as long as there is sunshine.

Spray Cover - a large form-fitted piece of material which covers the top of an open canoe to prevent swamping in large waves.

Spray Deck - the section of the spray deck which closes off the cockpit area of a kayak.

Standing Wave - a stationary wave normally found downstream of a rapid. It is generally caused by the collision of fast and slow moving water.

Stopper - a vertically circulating eddy of water which shows an area of upstream returning water on its surface.

Strainer - a mesh of submerged tree branches with the current flowing through it. Potentially a deadly situation.

S-turn - moving from one eddy to another across a tongue of water by using an eddy-in and eddy-out technique.

Tailrace - the outflow of water from hydro turbines as the water returns to its natural waterflow (i.e. into a lake or river).

Swell - the normally non-breaking roller coaster waves found when paddling ocean water.

Tide - the ebb and flow of the ocean's water surrounding our coast. Be sure to check local tide tables before setting out.

Tongue - a stream of fast water (usually slick black) between two eddies.

Trim - how the boat sits in the water. This can be affected by the position of paddler(s), equipment and paddler lean.

Undertow - on steep beaches the breaking wave is dumped on the beach by the force of gravity. The water from this wave then moves away from the beach under the next series of incoming waves. The power of the undertow in the coastal waters should be respected, as it has enough force to drag a person out to sea.

Wave - a hump of flowing water caused by the energy of the river as it changes direction or accelerates.

Weir - an artificial ledge creating a sudden fall on a river. Most of these appear rather tame and innocent but can be lethal. A word to the wise: keep your distance!

Reprint Credits

Every effort has been made to trace the ownership of all copyrighted selections used in this text and to make full acknowledgement for those used. If any copyrighted material has been used without permission or any error made in permission acknowledgement, it will be corrected in subsequent reprints.

Back, G. *Narrative of the arctic land expedition to the mouth of the Great Fish River.* Rutland: Charles E. Tuttle Co., 1836, 1970.

Cormack, W.E. *Narrative of A Journey Across the Island of Newfoundland.* London: Copp Clark Longman Ltd., 1928.

Cuff, Robert and Derek Wilton. *Jukes' Excursions.* St. John's: Harry Cuff Publications Limited, 1993.

Butler, Sir William Francis. *Wild Rivers.* Newfoundland and Labrador, Parks Canada, ARC Branch, planning division, Ottawa, 1977.

Bridges, Robert (ed.). *Poems of Gerald Manley Hopkins.* "Inversnaid," by Gerald Manley Hopkins. London: Oxford University Press, 1916.

Hubbard, Mina. *A Woman's Way Through Unknown Labrador.* St. John's: Breakwater Books Ltd., 1981.

Mason, Bill. *Path of the Paddle: An Illustrated Guide to the Art of Canoeing.* Toronto: Key Porter Books Limited, 1980.

Neary, Peter and Patrick O'Flaherty (eds.). *Social History of Canada Series, By Great Waters: A Newfoundland and Labrador Anthology,* "Selections from 1003 to the present". Excerpt from R.T.S. Lowell. Toronto: University of Toronto Press.

Newfoundland and Labrador, Government of, Department of Natural Resources. *Newfoundland and Labrador Traveller's Guide to the Geology,* 1994.

Oppersdorff, Tony. *Coastal Labrador: A Northern Odyssey.* Halifax: Nimbus Publishing Limited, 1991.

Wallace, Dillon. Lure of the Labrador Wild. St. John's: Breakwater Books Ltd., 1983.